CW01371810

A Gentleman's Guide to Duelling

Vincentio Saviolo's *Of Honour & Honourable Quarrels*

Edited and Presented by
Jared Kirby

Frontline Books, London

This book is dedicated to
my mother, Suzanne Kirby.
Honour would mean nothing without your example.

*A Gentleman's Guide to Duelling:
Vincentio Saviolo's Of Honour and Honourable Quarrels*

This edition published in 2013 by Frontline Books,
an imprint of Pen & Sword Books Ltd,
47 Church Street, Barnsley, S. Yorkshire, S70 2AS
www.frontline-books.com

Copyright © Jared Kirby, 2013

The right of Jared Kirby to be identified as the author of this work has been asserted by him in accordance with the Copyright, Designs and Patents Act 1988.

ISBN: 978-1-84832-527-2

All rights reserved. No part of this publication may be reproduced, stored in or introduced into a retrieval system, or transmitted, in any form, or by any means (electronic, mechanical, photocopying, recording or otherwise) without the prior written permission of the publisher. Any person who does any unauthorized act in relation to this publication may be liable to criminal prosecution and civil claims for damages.

CIP data records for this title are available from the British Library

For more information on our books, please visit
www.frontline-books.com, email info@frontline-books.com
or write to us at the above address.

Typeset in 11/15 point Italian Old Style by Wordsense Ltd, Edinburgh
Printed and bound by CPI Group (UK) Ltd, Croydon, CR0 4YY

Contents

List of Illustrations	vii
Acknowledgements	ix
Introduction	xi
Editor's Note	xvii
Part I: Biography of Vincentio Saviolo	**1**
The Man Behind the Words	3
Padua	5
The Military Man	8
Saviolo Jumps the Channel	11
Saviolo the Teacher	15
Finding Saviolo's School	19
Saviolo the Author	28
Saviolo's End	31
Saviolo's Legacy	32
Part II: Of Honour & Honourable Quarrels: The Second Book	**35**
The Preface	38
A Discourse of Single Combats with Some Necessary Considerations of the Causes for which they Are Undertaken	39
A Rule and Order Concerning the Challenger and Defender	66
A Conclusion Touching the Challenger and the Defender, and of the Wresting and Returning Back of the Lie, or Dementy	82
Of Injury, of the Charge, and of the Shame	104

Of the Inequality of Noblemen, and Chiefly of Commanding Lords	147
Touching the Satisfaction that Ought to be Made between Knights	161
The Nobility of Women	179
Appendices	191
Appendix A: A Transcription of the Section on Saviolo in Florio, *Second Frutes*	193
Appendix B: A Transcription of the Section on Saviolo in Silver, *Paradoxes of Defence*	197
Bibliography	203

Illustrations

Duel between Jarnac and Chateigneraie	42
A guard with the rapier	50
A rapier and dagger	50
Duel des mignons	56
A judicial duel	99
A knight entering the list for judicial combat	114
The knights and their attendants waiting for the combat to begin	114
This trial by combat begins with combatant on the right preparing to throw his spear	115
The combatant on the left throws his spear	115
The weapons of a man of arms	117
A combatant waiting for a decision	118
'Della due spade' (the two swords)	121
A sword and shield technique	121
'A prinse faut faire contre prinse comme est icy monstre par ce Lieutenant au Prevost'	125
Combat between man and dog	138
Duel de Bouteville	142

MAPS

1	The main thoroughfares within London in the area in which Bell Savage inn was situated	21
2	The area immediately around Bell Savage inn	22
3	The area of the sixteenth-century wells	25
4	A reconstruction of the friary in Blackfriars	27

Acknowledgements

I want to give a special thank you to Linda McCollum and Cecil Longino. Your constant revisions and support were invaluable. My name may be on this book, but it is just as much yours.

To my wife, Carol Kirby; your patience, love and support are unending. Thank you.

A big thank you to Sarah Goebler for a wonderful job rendering the maps in the biography of Saviolo.

I also want to thank the following people for their assistance and guidance: Maestro Ramon Martinez, Maestro Jeannette Acosta-Martinez, Russell Hogg, Steaphen Fick, Stephanie Zimmerman, Keena Suh, Mary Curtis, Tom Leoni, Ivan Peterson, Peter Nelson, Stephen Hand, Joseph Malit, Antone Blair, Val Eades, Danny Kirby, Tim Ruzicki, Michael Leventhal, Lionel Leventhal, Shulamit Kleinerman, Dee Cook, Cath Maloney, Rupert Meacher, John Lennox, Martin Reznick, Anthony Wade and Tony Mita.

The images on pages 42, 56, 114, 138 and 142 are reproduced courtesy of the Martinez Academy of Arms (www.martinez-destreza.com).

The sources of the other images are as follows:
Saviolo, V., *His Practise in Two Books, The First, Intreating of the Use of the Rapier and Dagger; The Second, Of Honour & Honourable Quarrels*, London, printed by John Wolfe, 1595: 50t, 50b.
Castle, Egerton, *Schools and Masters of Fence from the Middle Ages to the Eighteenth Century*, London, G. Bell & Sons, 1892: 99.
Talhoffers Fechtbuch aus dem Jahre 1467: Gerichtliche und Andere Zweikämpfe darstellend, Hrsg. von Gustav Hergsell, Prag, J. G. Calve, 1887. Rector, M. (ed. and trans.), *Medieval Combat: A Fifteenth-Century Illustrated Manual of Swordfighting and Close-Quarter Combat*, London, Greenhill Books, 2000: 114t, 114b, 115t, 115b.
Grassi, Giocomo di, *Ragione di adoprar sicuramente l'arme si da offesa come da difesa...*, Venetia, appresso G. Ziletti, 1570: 117, 121t.
Pistofilo, B., *Il torneo di Bonaventura Pistofilo nobile ferrarese dottor di legge e cavaliere nel Teatro di Pallade*, Bologna, Presso Clemente Ferroni, 1626: 118.

Acknowledgements

Agrippa, C., *Trattato Di Scientia d' Arme, con vn Dialogo di Filosofia di Camillo Aggrippa*, Rome, Blado, 1553: **121b**.

Didier, H. de St, *Traicté contenant les secrets du premier livre sur l'espée seule, mere de toutes armes*, Paris, Mettayer & Challenge, 1573: **125**.

Introduction

Who has not dreamt of knights, heroic deeds and chivalric quests? The fantastical notions of chivalry found in books and films are overflowing with romantic ideals of honour derived from stories such as Robin Hood and the Arthurian Round Table. Many people long to be brave, valiant, honest and true when they are young. I certainly wanted to be an infallible knight who rescued fair maidens from almost certain disaster. If only it were as simple as it sounded!

My interest in Vincentio Saviolo's life and work sprang from the desire to live an honourable life. It was simple as a boy; everything was so black and white. As I grew into adolescence this started to change. I found myself striving to make important decisions based on that youthful and unrefined notion of honourable behaviour. It quickly became apparent that the storybook version of honour was not as simple in real life. Bravery at its extreme (fearlessness) seemed opposed to reason and self-preservation. Constancy and kindness both shared little connection with honesty. I found my youthful shining armour tarnishing. How could I support a friend at all costs, even when they were in the wrong? Risking my well-being on altruistic actions now seemed unwise, and an honourable person should also behave wisely. My need to reconcile with this confusion and understand these concepts continued to grow as honour became a more complicated topic.

Attending university only fuelled my desire to understand this apparently self-contradictory ideal of honour. I met people on similar journeys and attempted to learn from their successes and failures. I read philosophy books and articles, and even wrote a research paper on honour. None of this clearly directed me in how to express the multifaceted aspects of honour. In modern life, honour

Introduction

seemed to hold only marginal value to most people. To merge these antiquated ideas with modern life, I started to explore much earlier works to find the roots of honour, virtue and etiquette. To my youthful amazement, the farther back I looked, the clearer the definitions of honour became, and I found more concrete examples of how honour and proper behaviour were interconnected.

Since then, I have found many examples of honourable and dishonourable behaviour during my years of historical and classical fencing. I first saw a clear historical context as to how honour should be expressed, and the necessity for doing so, when I read Saviolo's *Of Honour & Honourable Quarrels*.[*] In this work, the author records a sixteenth-century code of behaviour through anecdotes, commentary and legal references. This book gave me the perfect context in which to re-examine my thoughts on honour – not only in relation to my views over the years but also in regard to comments made by many philosophers going back to Aristotle in the fourth century BC.

While honour, virtue and even etiquette may be held as subjects grounded more in fancy than substance in today's society, it was certainly not the case for prominent Elizabethans. These matters had been well defined since antiquity and were of grave import to one's proper standing – not just in society but also in the very cosmos. A look at Aristotelian definitions of virtue, honour and human excellence guided me through Saviolo's treatise concerning honour.

Aristotle, in *Nicomachean Ethics*,[†] declares honour to be the greatest of the external goods. Because man is a social political

---

[*] Vincentio Saviolo, *Of Honour & Honourable Quarrels*, London, printed by John Wolfe, 1595. Saviolo's book was originally published as Vincentio Saviolo, *His Practise in Two Books*. The first book is Saviolo's treatise on the art of fencing. It is written as a dialogue between the Master (Saviolo) and his potential scholar (Luke). He teaches single rapier as well as rapier and dagger. A facsimile copy is available in James L. Jackson, *Three Elizabethan Fencing Manuals*, reprinted by Scholars' Facsimiles & Reprints, Ann Arbor, MI, 2001.

[†] For a good translation see Robert Williams (trans.), *The Nicomachean Ethics*

creature, human excellence is achieved through a public life, not a private one. The proper function of man is to flourish as a human being, and virtues are the habits needed to achieve this excellence. Mere fame is not the goal. Only the praise of other honourable men will serve as a public or outward acknowledgement of a great and virtuous man's inner value.

Consequently honour is the greatest award that the virtuous man may receive. Virtue is a state or balance between two vices (excess and deficiency). For example, the extremes of empty vanity and humility are balanced in the virtue of pride. The point of greatest virtue may not always reside in an exact midpoint between two extremes, though; sometimes it is closer to one extreme than the other. The virtuous (or good) person is not considered virtuous because he does good by accident but because he makes a conscious and informed choice to do so for the sole reason of doing good. In short, a good person deliberately chooses to do what is noble and right for its own sake.

Furthermore magnanimous people are more concerned with achieving human excellence than just doing good acts. They think themselves worthy of great things, and truly are, because virtuous people do not misjudge their own worth. They do not attempt to deceive either themselves or others of their inner value.

This understanding helped me empathise with Saviolo when he laments:

> What is become of the gentility and inbred courtesy of ancient noble gentlemen? Where is the magnanimity of the honourable knights of earlier times . . . ? Since all things fall to decay, it is no marvel though that virtue . . . is found but in a few. For surely there are many in whom nothing remains but the bare title of nobility.

---

of Aristotle, London, Longmans Green, 1869.

Introduction

The impetus to achieve true virtue, self-understanding and balance is what Saviolo finds lacking in his own time. This does not seem to have changed in four hundred years, as many people struggle with these same issues in the twenty-first century.

That is why a book such as this can be so helpful to a modern reader. Through example you can understand why these concepts are just as important today as they were in the times of Saviolo or Aristotle. But mere comprehension of these ideals is just the beginning. The excellent person is no couch potato. They act in accord with their knowledge and attempt to do great things. They understand their inner value is great, so they do not seek small tokens from simple people. They desire honours from other excellent people who have nothing greater to offer. Complete virtue is required for an excellent person, so magnanimity is the perfect state in which someone understands their own ability for complete virtue and knows they are both capable and worthy of achieving things beyond the average.

All of this is addressed or alluded to in *Of Honour & Honourable Quarrels*. While this work is a duelling code, it is important to understand the necessity and purpose of publishing it. The book does not promote or sanction personal violence between individuals. Rather it is a book of etiquette that extols the proper modes of behaviour expected between gentlemen of honour and virtue. Saviolo himself addresses man's inherent peaceful nature by describing the way God created man naked, without any natural weapons (contrary to other beasts of nature). *Of Honour & Honourable Quarrels* appeals to man's divine gift – that of reason – and admonishes him to uphold truth in both word and deed.

George Silver, an Englishman and public rival of Saviolo, gives us a quip about his character – that in the end Saviolo proved himself a better Christian than fencing master.* This may cast

---

* George Silver, *Paradoxes of Defence*, London, Edward Blount, 1599, p. 70. Exact quote is '. . . wherin he shewed himselfe a farre better man in his life, then

Introduction

doubt on Saviolo's abilities as a fencer, but it speaks volumes about his strength of character and shows the man attempting to live according to the same rules he has penned for proper gentlemanly behaviour. This comment can reassure us that his advice is not mere hypocritical fancy but a reasonable mode of maintaining honour, virtue and integrity.

Saviolo believes that the fencing master is also an arbiter on matters of punctilio, honour and deportment. By publishing this book Saviolo addresses those few remaining gentlemen who may, as necessity requires, have access to a well-defined process to defend their good names from base comments or actions that could potentially disrupt their personal balance of honour and cast doubt on their virtue. This process was only to be used to prove truth: '. . . and not to lay open a way for one man to revenge him of another. The punishment of such things rests in the prince . . .'.*

His duelling code sets down a methodical, reasonable and just means of achieving satisfaction between individuals who feel they have been wronged to such a severe extent that risking their very lives is the only way truth can be exposed from falsehood, thus preserving their reputations and honours. Not only does Saviolo explain the duelling process from beginning to end, but he also covers the legal ramifications when these protocols are not followed, who is allowed to duel whom and under what offences the duel is morally and honourably justifiable. With such detail, this book becomes an invaluable reflection of human behaviour and ideals in European traditions in the late sixteenth century.

Saviolo's treatise on duelling etiquette and the just defence of honour does more than simply record the most comprehensive duelling code written in English at that time. It expresses in minute detail the moral and social modes of behaviour by drawing

---

in his profession he was, for he professed armes, but in his life a better Christian.'
* Saviolo, *Of Honour & Honourable Quarrels*. See p. 106 of this book.

Introduction

upon traditional concepts of virtue and honour, which have been present in Western philosophy since antiquity. These concepts are just as relevant in the twenty-first century as they were in the sixteenth century or even in Ancient Greece and Rome. In fact they are needed now more than ever, as modern man has found it increasingly difficult to connect with these traditional concepts: for example, the way people hide behind anonymity on the internet and avoid responsibility for their words or deeds.

Saviolo's opus is of great importance to the amateur or professional historian, philosopher, legal scholar, Shakespearean expert and fencer too. *Of Honour & Honourable Quarrels* serves to help the fencer understand the gravity and seriousness that has served as the base of their art for hundreds of years. Meanwhile the historian will appreciate the thorough, first-hand account of Elizabethan aristocratic manners, and the philosopher can view this work as an excellent case study on applied ethics. Lawyers and legal scholars will be intrigued by the limits and accepted purview between criminal courts, civil courts and that of the *de facto* court of the *code duello*. Many elements of Shakespeare's plays become richer with an understanding of the duel, so any Shakespearean scholar would be wise to know this material.

As I continue striving to live an honourable life, I have found it crucial to have guideposts along the way. Saviolo's book is one of those. His words are not just whispers of some antiquated mode of social behaviour. They offer practical advice that can help you connect to the greater concept of honour, which is as useful in the twenty-first century as it was to the Elizabethans in 1595.

Jared Kirby, New York, 2013

Editor's Note

The natural ability to read and understand sixteenth-century English is a rare gift; many of the words and phrases hold archaic meanings that differ from their current usage. For many modern readers the works of William Shakespeare, Christopher Marlowe or Ben Jonson take considerable time, patience and footnotes to read and digest thoroughly. It can be difficult to find the amount of time required to tackle the works of these Elizabethan authors in our busy modern lives. Thus these brilliant pieces of literature, from one of the most prolific times in England's history, remain locked away, unattainable to the twenty-first-century reader.

This book has been created specifically to aid the modern reader in easily accessing Saviolo's treatise on the *code duello*. In it the original Elizabethan English text has been updated to modern grammatical conventions, spellings and sensibilities to make it more fluid reading. While the language has been updated, the spirit of the writing remains. Thus this book modernises the spelling of archaic words and adjusts the punctuation to meet current standards; it does not restructure Saviolo's original work nor greatly alter his original wording. For example, when Saviolo wrote: 'He resteth upon thine . . .' you will now read 'He rests upon your . . . .' Modern conjunctions have also been utilised to improve readability, and phrases such as 'now a daies' becomes 'nowadays' and 'any one' becomes 'anyone'. Possessive apostrophes have also been added where they were not in the original text.

Specific terms such as 'Armes' remain unchanged when they refer to weapons. Annotation has been added where it will aid understanding of what a sixteenth-century reader would have known when reading the treatise. There are many other interesting

Editor's Note

historical references in Saviolo's work (as well as side notes), but for the sake of brevity and so as not to detract from Saviolo's words they have not been included.

It is important to understand that the concept of Standard English, both in terms of orthography and pronunciation, was relatively alien to the Londoner of the late sixteenth century. Renaissance words had no fixed lexical definitions. The concept of defining words at all might have been strange to Shakespeare's contemporaries. They understood logical definition, which described what a thing is in the world. Dictionaries tended to explain words either by giving other signs corresponding to them, whether in English (synonyms) or in another language (translations), or by describing the reality to which they pointed. Where a modern reader would expect definitions, an Elizabethan reader would find illustrative sentences, idiomatic phrases, proverbs and chatty remarks about history or society.

Should you have the opportunity, ability, time and patience, I recommend reading Saviolo's book as it was originally written. Doing so will connect you to the English language usage of our past while offering additional insights into Saviolo's printed treatise and the layout of early modern printed texts. In the meantime this book is offered as a more palatable format, for easier digestion in which the wisdom of Saviolo's influential treatise is no longer locked away by archaic language and grammar. It is hoped that *Of Honour & Honourable Quarrels* will continue to motivate present and future generations to hold themselves accountable to a greater ideal of social etiquette and justice, as it did our ancestors when it was originally published.

Part I

Biography of Vincentio Saviolo

The Man Behind the Words

Vincentio Saviolo was arguably the most influential fencing master in Elizabethan England. He exposed a xenophobic English society to Italian thought, ideals and notions of justice through his books on fencing, honour and the duel. Saviolo's presence alone created a stir in London, but his social influence reached beyond that of his fencing school or his aristocratic students and friends, through to the writings of popular playwrights and pamphleteers of the day. The English writers began a common mimicking or mocking of Italian terms, points of honour and duelling, all of which are the direct focus of Saviolo's notable work – *His Practise in Two Books*. Thomas Lodge, John Marston, Ben Jonson, Thomas Kyd and especially William Shakespeare were all affected by this publication to some extent. No other fencing master had such a tremendous influence on the art and literature of the Elizabethan era.

Compiling a biography of Saviolo is a difficult task due to the lack of information on his life. It is important to note that, while there are many secondary sources describing Saviolo's life, much of this information is unsubstantiated and can often be traced back to earlier unsubstantiated sources. In the beginning of this biography project, I was shocked to find much of what is recorded about Saviolo was not necessarily true. This motivated me to search for as much primary source and verifiable information as I could find. Unfortunately there is very little, and most of it comes directly from Saviolo's own accounts. However there were two contemporary writers – John Florio and George Silver – who provided supplementary information on Saviolo's character.

John Florio was a well-known Italian who helped to popularise the Italian language among the young English gallants of the day, with his phrase books and Italian–English dictionaries. Although Florio was born in England, he fled with his parents to Switzerland after Mary I ascended to the throne in 1553. He returned to England after Elizabeth I came to power in 1558. His popular phrase books consisted of a series of dialogues between a young gentleman, his servant and several friends. The narratives cover many subjects, from items found in one's bedchamber to plays and fencing practice (where Florio mentions Saviolo as 'V. S.').

The second supplementary source was an outspoken English gentleman by the name of George Silver. In his two works – *Paradoxes of Defence* and *Brief Instructions upon my Paradoxes of Defence*[*] – Silver gives a number of disparaging anecdotes concerning Saviolo, and he also criticises several other contemporary Italian fencing masters residing in London. The first book was published in 1599, while historians believe the second – a manuscript discovered long after Silver's death – was written early in the reign of James I.[†] It is ironic that Silver left a fair number of anecdotes and information about his Italian nemesis – the foreigner he attempted to injure or kill at sword's point. Without Silver's writings much of Saviolo's story would have been lost.

This biography will place Saviolo's contributions within the context of his time, as recorded in period primary sources, while augmenting previous facts and information with new research I have uncovered. As well as clarifying any misnomers or inaccurate

---

[*] George Silver, *Brief Instructions upon my Paradoxes of Defence*, nd. Eventually published in C. G. R. Matthey (ed.), *The Works of George Silver: Comprising 'Paradoxes of Defence' and 'Bref Instructions upon My Paradoxes of Defence'*, London, George Bell, 1898.

[†] 1603–25.

information propagated by earlier scholars, this biography will combine all the currently known primary references into one book to assist future scholars and historians in continuing to delve into the life of this fascinating individual.

Padua

In *His Practise in Two Books: The First, Intreating of the Use of the Rapier and Dagger; The Second, Of Honour & Honourable Quarrels,*[*] Saviolo asserts he is from the northern Italian town of Padua (Padova), which is in the Veneto region of Italy. This is also confirmed by Florio, in *Second Frutes*, in the form of a dialogue between two gentlemen discussing one master, V. S., who teaches rapier in London:

> G. What place in Italie was he borne in?
> E. I take him to be a padoan.[†]

Saviolo recounts a number of stories about the bravery and skill of his fellow Paduans, so he seemed very proud of his home and countrymen. This should not be surprising given Padua's rich history.

In the *Aeneid*, the Roman poet Virgil describes Padua as having been founded by the Trojan prince Antenor, after the fall of Troy

---

[*] Vincentio Saviolo, *His Practise in Two Books: The First, Intreating of the Use of the Rapier and Dagger; The Second, Of Honour & Honourable Quarrels*, London, printed by John Wolfe, 1595.

[†] John Florio, *Florios Second Frutes, to be Gathered of Twelve Trees, of Divers but Delightsome Tastes to the Tongues of Italians and Englishmen. To which is Annexed his Gardine of Recreation Yeelding Six Thousand Italian Proverbs*, London, Thomas Woodcock, 1591, p. 119.

in 1183 BC. This mythological beginning certainly plays a key role in connecting the city to antiquity, and it served as a point of pride among Padua's citizens through the sixteenth century, if not much earlier. By 1222 the city had been able to boast an established university (Padua University), whose motto, 'Universa Universis Patavina Libertas',* reflected a strong desire to provide liberty in education. Accordingly the university attracted many outstanding professors during the sixteenth century, the most famous of whom was Galileo Galilei. With a major university offering a measure of freedom in its curriculum beyond that offered by its rivals, Padua was a large draw for the intellectual elite of the time. This influx of students and professors from all over Europe meant the city of Padua was a busy hub of intellectual, philosophical, scientific and social activity. Saviolo recounts a story from his youth about the university: 'At Padua where I was born, in my time was a gentlewoman of good reckoning who professed the civil law publicly. She came daily into the colleges and schools and disputed with all the doctors and scholars of the university.'†

A search through the state archives of Padua (Archivio di Stato di Padova) for any official records of a Vincentio (Vincenzio) Saviolo, Saviola or Savioli (the Latin variation of Saviolo) between the years of 1550 and 1603 provides no evidence regarding the birth or legal existence of Vincentio Saviolo. There are no extant records of Vincentio Saviolo owning property in Padua, serving in the local militia as infantry, cavalry, artillery or as a grenadier. However, despite the lack of information on Vincentio himself, the state archives do point to the parish of San Giorgio, also referred to as San Zorzo, as being the specific parish of Padua from where the family name Saviolo descended. Unfortunately there are no parish baptismal records available prior to the 1580s for all of San

---

* Translation: 'Complete liberty for all at Padua University'.
† Saviolo, *Of Honour & Honourable Quarrels*. See p. 188 of this book.

Giorgio parish. Discovering Saviolo's exact date of birth is now virtually impossible. This did not stop a search though. Looking through other references of the period I found that the *Dizionario Storico-Blasonico*[*] confirms the Latin variant of Saviolo's surname as a prominent seventeenth-century Paduan family:

> Savioli of Padua. Involved since 1626 with the Nobles' Council of Padua, their nobility was confirmed by sovereign edict in Sept. 1818. A Ducal edict on Jan. 27 1796 (from Doge Manin), they were adorned with the title of count, as descendants of one of the brothers Antonio, Annibale and Lodovico Gassan, to whom this same title was given by John III King of Poland with a diploma on Apr. 17, 1682. – COAT OF ARMS: split; in one half, silver feathering, with on each feather a tuft of ermine hair; in the other half, light blue and golden stripes.[†]

Another book in the state archives of Padua, *Alfabetto Citta*,[‡] from 1575, shows all Saviolos listed as being persons of merit and social standing, such as property owners, public notaries, doctors of law and soldiers. While we may never know when Saviolo was born, it is clear that the Saviolo name denotes a worthy family.

---

[*] G. B. di Crollalanza, *Dizionario Storico-Blasonico delle famiglie nobili e notabili Italiane estinte e fiorenti compilato dal commendatore G.B. di Crollalanza*, Vol. 2 L–S, Pisa, Pisa Presso la direzione del giornale Araldico, 1888, p. 497.

[†] Translation courtesy of Tom Leoni. Original Italian is: '*Savioli di Padova: Aggregata fin dal 1626 al Consiglio nobile di Padova, fu confermata nella sua nobiltà con sovrana risoluzione 4 Sett. 1818. Con ducale 27 Gen. 1796 del Doge Manin, fu anche decorate del titolo di conte come discendente da uno dei fratelli Antonio, Annibale e Lodovico Bassan, ai quail fu conferito questo titolo da Giovanni III Re di Polonia con diploma 17 Apr. 1682. – ARMA: Spaccato; nel 4.[*] piumettato d'argento, ciascuna piuma caricata di una mosca di armellino di nero; nel 2º. Bandito d'azzurro e d'oro.*'

[‡] There are no author, editor or publisher/printer details for *Alfabetto Citta*. The only way to get access is to go to the state archives of Padua and talk to the curator.

The Military Man

Saviolo was exposed to soldiering at a young age. Military service to one's prince and nation was an expected duty of a gentleman, so this was not unusual. In the final chapter of *Of Honour & Honourable Quarrels* Saviolo mentions a boyhood friend who was the son of a trumpeter for a Venetian regiment:

> I remember when I was a youth, a friend of mine, son to a trumpet in pay under the captains of the Signorie of Venice, was with a certain cousin set upon by eleven other young men who were their enemies. His mother perceiving this took a partisan in her hands and defended her son and cousin and sorely wounded five of their enemies and made the rest fly.*

Not only does this passage highlight the message of the entire chapter (on the nobility of women) but it also depicts a young Saviolo growing up around military families.

All through his books, Saviolo paints a picture that he is well travelled through the European continent and familiar with military exploits. For example, he mentions that he served in various military campaigns against the Turks in Slovenia and Croatia.† He recounts the details of the armour and weapons used in Croatia: 'At the assault he bare in his hand a kind of pickaxe . . . This kind of weapon is much used by the Slavonians, Croatians, Turks, Albanians and Hungarians.'‡ He describes numerous accounts of duels and military accomplishments by well-known

---

* Saviolo, *Of Honour & Honourable Quarrels*. See p. 183 of this book.
† Saviolo, *Of Honour & Honourable Quarrels*. See p. 176 of this book.
‡ Saviolo, *Of Honour & Honourable Quarrels*. See p. 59 of this book.

The Military Man

captains including Ascanio della Cornia[*] (master of the camp for the army of Don Juan of Austria) and Marco Querini[†] (captain of the galleys for the Seigniory of Venice). Saviolo asserts that he received extensive training in the use of the sword, but never mentions the name of any of his teachers:

> Since my childhood I have seen very many masters the which have taken great pains in teaching, and I have marked their diverse manners of play and endangering: wherefore (both for the particular contentment & pleasure of the Gentlemen my friends, and for the general help & benefit of many) I have changed five or six sundry manner of plays, taught to me by diverse masters, and reduced them unto one by my no little labour and pain, and in this will I resolve you, and give you therein so direct a rule and instruction, as that thereby (being my scholar) you may attain unto the perfect knowledge of this science.[‡]

The fragments gathered on Saviolo's early years create an image of a young gentleman from a prominent Paduan family who had the opportunity for an excellent education.[§] He received extensive training in fencing and gained practical military experience against

---

[*] Cornia (correctly spelt Corgna) was one of the most famous men in Europe in the sixteenth century. He was a master of arms and an invincible swordsman. Three thousand people travelled from Rome, Florence, Siena and Perugia to see his duel with Giannetto Taddei. He was a military engineer who took part in almost all the wars of the period. He died in 1571 from wounds received at the Battle of Lepanto, and a nine-day funeral was held before he was buried in Perugia at the Della Corgna Chapel in the Church of St Francis.

[†] Querini was captain of the galley for the Seigniory of Venice, which played a large part in the war with the Turks and was also at Lepanto. He is credited in 1570 with the only successful move made by the Venetians, when he destroyed the Turkish fortress at Brazzo de Maina on the southeast coast of Morea. He is continually referred to as 'Captain of the Gulf' (Adriatic).

[‡] Saviolo, *His Practise in Two Books*, Book 1, p. 5, verso.

[§] This is clear from Saviolo's understanding of things such as Aristotle's *Nicomachean Ethics*.

the Turks in Croatia, making him well travelled and well read. Several years after Saviolo's arrival in England John Florio fortifies this image of Saviolo in *Second Frutes*.

> G. But to come to our purpose again, of whom do you learn to play at your weapon?
> E. Of master V. S.
> G. Who, that Italian that looks like Mars himself?
> E. The very same.
> G. Does he play well? Has he good skill in his weapon?
> E. As much as any other man.
> G. Is he valiant and a tall man of his hands?
> E. More valiant than a sword itself.
> G. I have heard him reported to be a notable tall man.
> E. He will hit any man, be it with a thrust or *stoccata*, with an *imbroccata* or a charging blow, with a right or reverse blow, be it with the edge, with the back or with the flat, even as it likes him.
> G. Is he left or right handed?
> E. Both, all is one to him.
> G. What does he commonly take a month?
> E. But little and there is no man that teaches with more dexterity and nimbleness than he.
> G. Can he doo nothing else, but play at fence?
> E. Yes, he hath good skill in every kind of weapon, he shoots well in a piece, he shoots well in great ordinance and besides he is a very excellent good soldier.
> G. All these rare good qualities do very seldom times concur in any one of our fencers.
> E. Moreover, he is a good dancer, he dances very well, both galliards, and pavins, he vaults most nimbly and capers very loftily.
> G. He differs very much from other fencers.

E. Yet there are many honest and proper men among them.
G. There be some but one swallow brings not summer, nor one devil makes not hell.
E. Is he a great quarreller, and a brawler?
G. He is most patient, nether does he go about to revenge any injury that is offered him, unless it touch his credit and honour very far.*

Through this dialogue Florio bolsters the image of Saviolo being a brave skilled and valiant soldier. He is able to handle not only a sword with exceeding skill but also the other weapons of a soldier's profession. More importantly Florio is careful to clarify that Saviolo is no brawler or common ruffian but a good dancer, honest, patient and graceful; in short he has all the fine qualities required of a courteous gentleman.

Saviolo Jumps the Channel

It is unclear exactly why Saviolo chose to make his way to England around 1587, but a strong possibility lies in the prospects available to an Italian gentleman in England at the time. It is undeniable that under Elizabeth I's reign, Italian fashion, manners and customs were heavily imported into London along with foreign dance, music, language and fencing instructors. From her youth, Elizabeth had Italian tutors and was well versed in Italian, along with a number of other languages. The queen once remarked to the Archduke of Wurttemberg: 'I love the manners and ways of Italy; I am half

---

* Florio, *Second Frutes*, pp. 117, 119; see also p. 193 of this book for original text.

Italian myself (*me semble que je suis demie Italiene*)." Bizarrely the comment was made in French. While Elizabeth's court was freely visited by Italians, it was her grandfather, Henry VII, who had opened the door for the invasion of Italian cultural influence by expanding commercial trade with Italian seaports. Trade soon led to the establishment of Italian banks in London, and from that point Italian influence gradually continued to grow.

By Elizabeth's reign, the English aristocracy was well primed to receive the influx of foreign manners and odd implements as they stepped farther away from their earlier history of isolationism. Two items that had earlier become commonplace in many European courts were introduced to Englishmen in the late sixteenth century – the drinking glass and the dinner fork. William Harrison, an English chronicler, lamented:

> It is a world to see in these our days, wherein gold and silver most abounds, how that our gentility, as loathing those metals because of the plenty, do now generally choose rather the Venice glasses, both for our wine and beer, than any of those metals (because of the plenty), or stone wherein beforetime we have been accustomed to drink . . .[†]

With the English nobility eager to take on foreign affectations, it is no surprise to find Saviolo making his way to England with all the potential that resided in its growing capital, London. By the close of the sixteenth century, Londoners were proving to have a voracious appetite for the printed word. Broadsheets of new ditties and ballads were continually being peddled for a penny or two. Pamphleteers such as Robert Greene kept themselves busy

---

[*] Mary Augusta Scott, *Elizabethan Translations from the Italian*, Boston & New York, Houghton Mifflin, 1916, pp. xxxvii, xxxviii.

[†] William Harrison, *The Description of England: The Classic Contemporary Account of Tudor Social Life by William Harrison*; edited by Georges Edelen, New York, Dover, 1994, p. 128.

distributing information on subjects ranging from classifying the degrees of vagrants and criminals to denouncing the new, up-and-coming playwright or upstart crow, William Shakespeare.[‡] In this atmosphere the publishers of London were continually on the lookout for new material to print; they even turned to translating foreign works to help fill the Elizabethans' ravenous literary appetite. By the final quarter of the sixteenth century London was home to more than eight Italian translators such as John Florio actively publishing works into English.

During this period many Italian works were made available in English for the first time. Topics ranging from theology, science, rhetoric, military arts and plays all found their way through the busy London printing presses to the hands of an eager English audience. Some 230 separate Italian titles were translated between 1540 and 1600.[§] Some of the more familiar titles are *The Tragical History of Romeus and Juliet* by Matteo Bandello, *The Art of Riding* by Claudio Corte, *His True Art of Defence* by Giacomo di Grassi and *The Courtier* by Baldassare Castiglione.

While not a translation but an original work written in English, Saviolo's book helped fill the Elizabethans' desire for new and foreign literature. Saviolo dedicates his book to Robert Devereux, the 2nd Earl of Essex, a favourite of Elizabeth I. Essex's position and military service allowed him to be well travelled through Europe. He served in the Netherlands from 1585 to 1586 and was knighted for gallantry. He participated in additional campaigns against the Spanish and distinguished himself during the capture and burning of Cádiz. Devereux was quite the ambitious young English nobleman. Such a world traveller in the Elizabethan court would certainly have been well acquainted with the popular Italian fashion

---

‡ Robert Greene, *Greenes Groats-worth of Witte, Bought with a Million of Repentance*, New York, Burt Franklin, 1970, pp. 45–6.

§ Scott, *Elizabethan Translations*.

do was play his prize for Master. Bonetti refused. He was an Italian gentleman while the London Masters were common Englishmen. Therefore he had no desire to be associated with them.

Bonetti continued his travels, but in 1584 he took up residence in part of the Blackfriars after acquiring the lease from John Lyly.[*] He spent a great sum of money on renovations, but never got a chance to finish. By November 1585 Bonetti was imprisoned for disobeying an order of chancery.[†] The length of his incarceration is not known, but Bonetti died in 1587.[‡] He left a partially remodelled college of fence and his 'boy', Jeronimo. Never using a last name, George Silver describes Jeronimo as *'Signior Rocko his boy, that taught Gentlemen in the Blacke-Fryers*, as Usher for his maister in steed of a man'.[§] When Saviolo came to England Jeronimo started to teach with him. They did this for approximately seven to eight years, according to Silver.[¶]

Saviolo most likely had come to England in 1587 (and certainly before 1589).[**] He inherited many of Bonetti's problems with

---

[*] This is strange because one year prior to this Bonetti had registered a complaint against the Earl of Oxford's men. Lyly was one of the Earl of Oxford's men, and one source even called Lyly his protégé (Irwin Smith, *Shakespeare's Blackfriars Playhouse*, New York, New York University Press, 1964). There seems eventually to have been a separation between Oxford and Lyly, which may have started around this time.

[†] Linda McCollum, 'Dispelling Myths about the Early History of Rapier Fencing in England', *Spada II: An Anthology of Swordsmanship*, Highland Village, TX, The Chivalry Bookshelf, 2005, p. 25.

[‡] 'Rocko Bonetto' is assessed every year in the Second Lay Subsidy at vj.li. xij.s. from 1583 to 1587, when there is a note in the margin stating 'Dead in Thospitall'. Aylward, p. 49.

[§] Silver, *Paradoxes*, p. 64. Records for Blackfriars district make no mention of Jeronimo or Saviolo.

[¶] 'Then came Vincentio and Jeronimo, they taught rapier fight at the court, at London, and in the country, by the space of seven or eight years or thereabouts.' Silver, *Paradoxes*, p. 66.

[**] A census to record every foreigner in London was issued on 6 March 1593. Record 929 was 'Saviolo, Vincenzia, 1; Italian, born in Venice; no occupation; no children; no stranger maid servant; dwelt in England 6 years; no denizen; of

members of the Masters of Defence, and with Silver in particular. In response to a comment attributed to Saviolo and Jeronimo about the English stepping back too much in the fight, George Silver and his brother Toby issued a challenge to the two Italians to prove once and for all which was better.* The Silvers did not get an answer from the Italians before they printed up the handbills and were quite embarrassed when the Italians did not show. Silver later accused the Italians of cowardice since Bell Savage was 'within a bow shot of their fence school' so there was no obvious reason for the Italians' lack of attendance.

Silver also tells that two to three days later Saviolo and Jeronimo had an encounter with members of the London Masters. As Saviolo and Jeronimo were passing through a hall to go to their school, the Masters of Defence invited them for a drink. Silver says: '...the Italians being very cowardly, were afraid, and presently drew their rapiers. There was a pretty wench standing by, that loved the Italians. She ran with outcry into the street: "Help! Help! The Italians are like to be slain." '† People ran into the house

---

the Italian Church; keeps one English man servant and one maid servant; sets no English person to work.' Chris Chatfield, 'Stranger 929,' 2010; http://www.the1595.com/documents/STRANGER-929.pdf (accessed August 2013). This would put his arrival in London at 1587.

* 'These two Italian fencers, especially Vincentio, said Englishmen were strong men, but had no cunning, and they would go back too much in their fight, which was great disgrace unto them. Upon these words of disgrace against Englishmen, my brother Toby Silver and myself made challenge against them both, to play with them at the single rapier, rapier and dagger, the single dagger, the single sword, the sword and target, the sword and buckler, & two hand sword, the staff, battle axe, and Morris pike, to be played at the Bell Savage upon the scaffold, where he that went in his fight faster back than he ought, of Englishmen or Italian, should be in danger to break his neck off the scaffold. We caused to that effect, five or six score bills of challenge to be printed, and set up from Southwarke to the Tower, and from thence throughout London unto Westminster, we were at the place with all these weapons at the time appointed, within a bow shot of their fence school.' Silver, *Paradoxes*, p. 66.

† Silver, *Paradoxes*, p 67.

and parted the fray. Evidently this only helped add to the Italians' prestige in court.

The final story that Silver mentions about Saviolo is his confrontation with another English master – Bartholomew Bramble. When Saviolo was in the county of what was then known as Somersetshire, Bramble challenged him to play with rapier and dagger. Saviolo is reported to have replied: 'If I play with thee, I will hit thee 1, 2, 3, 4 thrusts in the eie together', and later, when Bramble would not relent, Saviolo retorted: 'by God me scorn to play with thee'.* Bramble was so incensed by Saviolo's attitude that he boxed Saviolo on the ear and knocked him down. Fearing Saviolo's response, Bramble reached for a blackjack,† half full of beer. Saviolo fingered his dagger and claimed that he could have Bramble thrown into jail for his actions. The Englishman, in turn, called Saviolo a coward and poured the rest of the beer on him. Saviolo again refused to respond to the provocation, since Bramble had no weapon other than the blackjack. When he met Bramble on the street the next day, the Italian bought him a present of a dozen silken points‡ from a mercer's shop, and promised to teach him how to thrust farther than his fellow Englishmen. Silver finishes the story by calling Saviolo a better Christian than a fighter. After this, for more than a page and a half, he criticises Saviolo's book on rapier and dagger.

---

* Silver, *Paradoxes*, p. 69.
† A leather pitcher.
‡ 'And the Venetian-hosen, they reach beneath the knee to the gartering place to the Leg, where they are tied finely with silk points, or some such like.' Phillip Stubbes and Frederick J. Furnivall, *Phillip Stubbes's Anatomy of Abuses in England in Shakspere's Youth, A.D. 1583: Part II: The Display of Corruptions Requiring Reformation*, London, Trübner, 1882, p. 56.

Finding Saviolo's School

The location of Saviolo's fencing school has long eluded scholars as there are few clues to its exact location in London. I have been searching intermittently for more than fifteen years to find where it might have stood. With much of the recorded history of this particular area destroyed in the Great Fire of 1666, research has been difficult. There are only four extant reference points available to use in attempting to pinpoint the school's position. They are as follows: his school was 'at the signe of the red Lyon',[*] 'in the little striate, where the well is'.[†] Additionally the 'fence school' was 'within a bow shot'[‡] of Bell Savage sometime between 1587 and 1598.

In the following section each data point along with its significance and historical connection will be examined in greater detail. Thanks to the modern ease of access to information and the research presented here, there is now a clearer idea of where Saviolo probably held his classes in the art and science of fencing.

⇥≡◯⇤

'WITHIN A BOW SHOT' OF BELL SAVAGE

The Bell Savage Inn was a popular site for prize playing and also served as an occasional playhouse. In fact Wheatley's *London Past and Present* (1891)[§] mentions that 'Here in Queen Elizabeth's time,

---

[*] Florio, *Second Frutes*, p. 117.
[†] Florio, *Second Frutes*, p. 117.
[‡] Silver, *Paradoxes*, p. 67.
[§] H. B. Wheatley, *London Past and Present: Its Histories, Associations, and Traditions, Based upon the Handbook of London by the Late Peter Cunningham*, London, Murray, 1891, p. 155.

was a school of defence', but says nothing further and unfortunately does not reference the information. The inn was located on Ludgate Hill due west of St Paul's Cathedral but before Fleet Ditch. It was northwest and just across the street from the Blackfriars parish.

It is unclear how the inn came to be named Bell Savage. It seems that the original sign of the house was the Bell, but a deed from the fifteenth century speaks of 'all the tenement or inn with its appurtenances, called Savage's inn, otherwise called the Bell on the Hoop'.* This Savage's Bell could have easily become known as Bell Savage. It was also spelled *Belle Sauvage* and is rumoured to have been named after Pocahontas when she came to London (*La Belle Sauvage* translates as 'The Savage Beauty'). The landlord's tokens displayed an Indian woman holding a bow and arrow, and the inn's sign was a savage man standing by a bell, so this story may have a little truth in it. However this building gained its name, it is a crucial point to locating Saviolo's fencing school.

When George Silver issued his challenge to Saviolo it was to 'be played at the Bell Savage . . . within a bow shot of their fence school'. Map 1 shows where Bell Savage once stood within the city of London.

Modern research has ascertained that the maximum range of a bow shot at that time was approximately 225 yards (206 m).† Armed with this information and measurement, the position of Saviolo's school can be estimated by creating a circumference of 225

---

* Henry C. Shelley, *Inns and Taverns of Old London*; http://www.buildinghistory.org/primary/inns/inns.shtml (accessed August 2013).

† There were two types of arrows: war arrows and 'prick' (target) arrows. War arrows were heavier than target arrows. They had heavier heads and were fletched with larger feathers. Average length of the bow from the *Mary Rose* shipwreck is 6 ft 2 in (1.8 m). A bow this size could shoot a 30-inch arrow 200 yards (183 m) . An estimated 100-lb (45-kg) draw weight at 30 inches (75 cm) is needed to send a war arrow 200 yards (183 m). The *Mary Rose* bows have been estimated to range from 80 lb (36 kg) to 170 lb (77 kg), although the top weight might be questioned. Robert Hardy, *Longbow: A Social and Military History*, Cambridge, Stephens, 1976.

Finding Saviolo's School

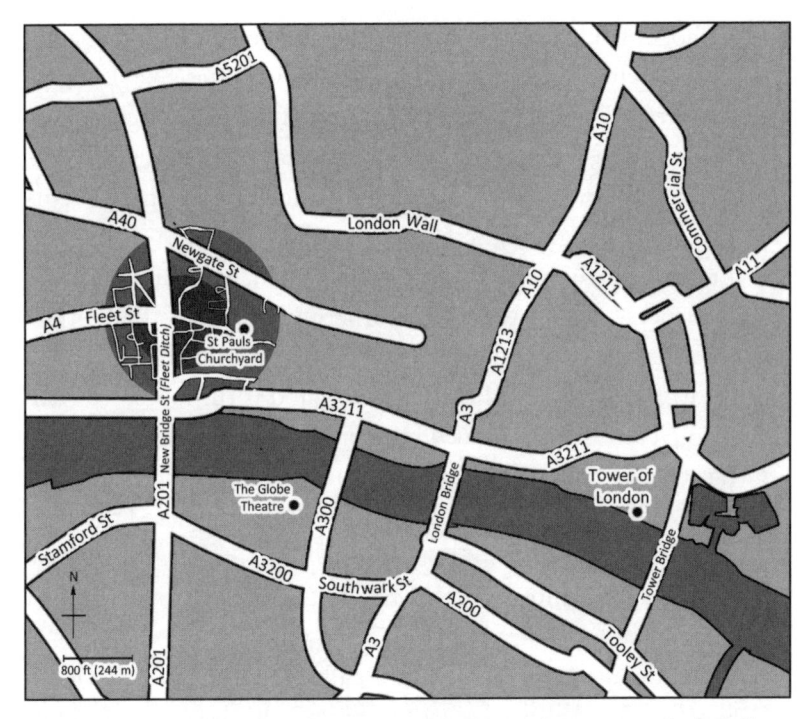

Map 1: *The main thoroughfares within London in the area in which Bell Savage inn was situated. (The old street names have been added in italics after their modern equivalents.)*

yards (206 m) around Bell Savage (see map 2). This area includes the parishes of St Ann/Blackfriars, St Bride and St Martin Ludgate.

When walking around this area you will find that it is really quite small. It was a ten-minute walk from Bonetti's first 'College' in Warwick Lane to his school in Blackfriars. It only took fifteen minutes to walk from Belle Savage to any of the extremities of the map 2 circle (see p. 22). Saviolo's school must have been within the area of this circle, so next the remaining data points were researched with this in mind.

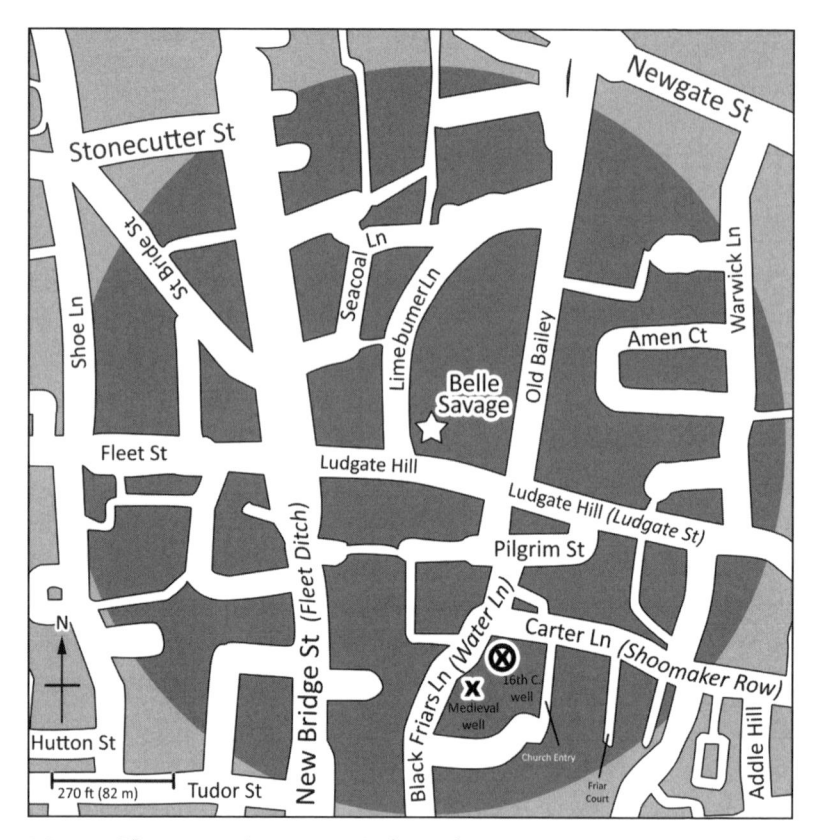

Map 2: *The area within 225 yards (206 m) of Bell Savage inn is indicated by the darkened part on this map.*

'AT THE SIGNE OF THE RED LYON'

The best resource to find a sign in London is Bryant Lillywhite's 1972 book *London Signs*.* Within its 700 pages is the section on Red Lion, which starts with: 'The RED LION is one of the most popular of inn and tavern signs throughout Britain.' He was not joking; there are 206 entries for Red Lion/Lyon. That figure

---

* Bryant Lillywhite, *London Signs: A Reference Book of London Signs from Earliest Times to About the Mid-Nineteenth Century, etc.*, London, George Allen & Unwin, 1972.

increases by another fifty-two entries of Lyon/Lion. Knowing that Saviolo's school had to be near Bell Savage reduced that list of 258 to a little over a dozen entries, for taverns within 1,000 yards (914 m) of Bell Savage yard (after all it is quite possible that 'within a bow shot' was a colloquialism and not meant to be taken as an exact measurement).

Past scholars have suggested a couple of possibilities such as that 'Red Lyon Street existed in Holborn, which was northwest of St Paul's and was noted for the numerous springs in the area'* and 'At the signe of the Red Lyon, in the little striate [Watling] where the well is.'† Both of these are more than 1,000 yards (914 m) away and can be ruled out as serious possibilities.

Looking at the Red Lion signs that were literally within a bow shot of Belle Savage narrowed it down to two final options. The first was cited as '#12179: Red Lyon Inn Fleet Strete [sic] 1571–1666'. A small part of Fleet Street is within the area around Bell Savage, but Fleet Street is very long and without a cross street this reference was of little value in our search. It was also a prominent street and therefore failed to meet the criteria of 'little' (which is one of our other clues). The Guildhall Library houses a sixteenth-century title deed that referenced a Red Lion sign in Black Horse Alley (which was within a bowshot of Bell Savage). This would place it in the parish of St Bridget's/Brides and is quite possibly where the Red Lyon Inn was. That could be considered a little street, but no well could be found.

The other citation within range was '#12307 – Red Lion Cock Lane, West Smithfield, Before 1677'. While Cock Lane had a water conduit at the end of it, there is no map of that time that identifies any wells.

---

* McCollum, fn. 61.

† Jay P. Anglin, 'The Schools of Defence in Elizabethan London', *Renaissance Quarterly*, Vol. 37, No. 3 (Autumn 1984), p. 408.

It was slightly disheartening to go through all these references and still fall short of a reliable match within the sphere around Bell Savage. That said, it is quite possible that the reference needed for the sign of Saviolo's school went up in the flames of 1666. I continued to search in hopes of finding a location that matched at least three of the four data points.

'. . . IN THE LITTLE STRIATE, WHERE THE WELL IS'

Despite poring over many maps of the area around Bell Savage from the fifteenth century to modern times, it was very difficult to find a 'little street'. The maps of the fifteenth and sixteenth centuries did not go into enough detail, and moreover the area changed considerably after the Great Fire. If the street was truly so little, it makes sense that it may not even appear on an early map or could have disappeared in the rebuild.

By working only within the area of the circle presented in map 2, a well should have been an easier find. Easier, yes, but by no means easy. The earlier mention of a well in Watling Street cannot be correct as that is more than 1,000 yards (914 m) away from Bell Savage, which is much farther than a 'bowshot.'

I kept researching the area around Bell Savage and contacted many of the old London guilds. Dee Cook, the archivist for the Society of Apothecaries, was an invaluable help. She had heard of a dig that uncovered an old well somewhere in the area, though she could not give me specifics as to the exact location.

With this in mind, I went to the Museum of Archaeology to find out which dig uncovered the sixteenth-century well and discovered that it was possibly a post-medieval well that was filled in between 1680 and 1730 (therefore in use prior to 1680). It was

Finding Saviolo's School

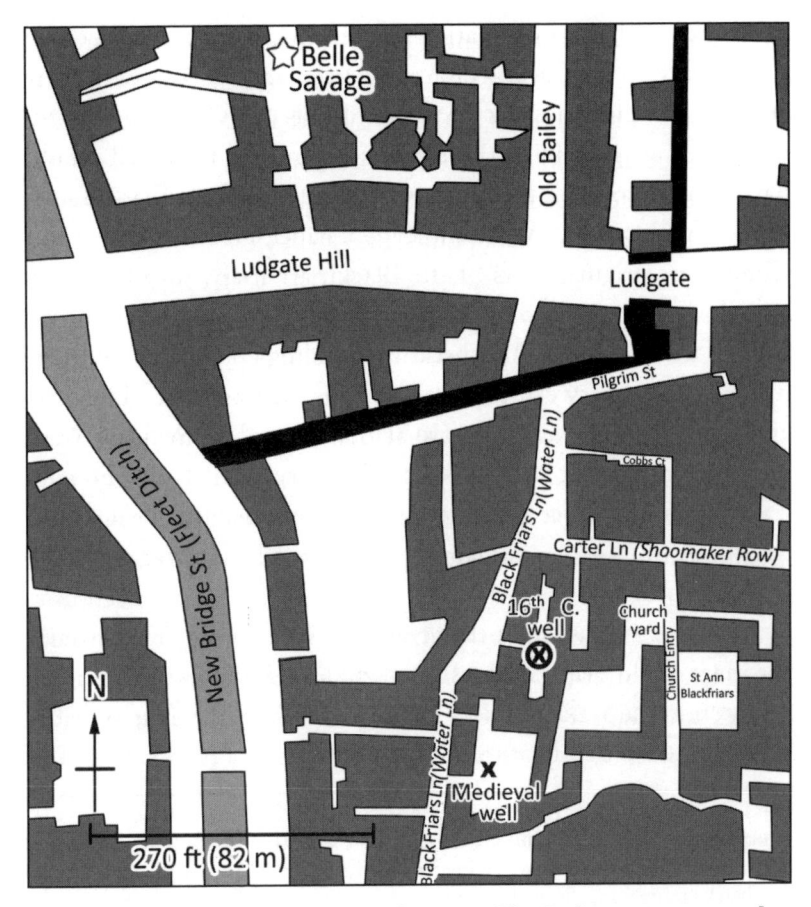

Map 3: *This is based on a 1676 London map. The ⊗ shows approximately where the well would have been. The × a little lower down is the site of a medieval well in the courtyard of the Society of Apothecaries.*

approximately 150 yards (137 m) from Bell Savage and is shown in maps 2 and 3.*

---

* The report detailed the following: 'Its uppermost surviving portion consisted of coursed trapezoidal tiles and large chalk flocks bonded in a light buff hard mortar with frequent flecks of lime, while lower down it consisted of bricks. The unusual shape of the tiles created a well-crafted circle in plan, measuring 0.75 m. across internally and 1.17 m. overall. It was impossible to record the

Armed with this information from the Museum of Archaeology I went back to the Society of Apothecaries and worked with their archivist to pinpoint the location of this 'newly sprung' well, uncovered at the end of the twentieth century. This well would have been just outside the north wall of the Blackfriars friary Guest-House (see map 4). While the Lady Chapel, Preaching Nave and Choir were original parts of the Blackfriars friary, they had been torn down (represented by the heavy black lines), so that the north wall of the Society of Apothecaries' building (purchased by them in 1632) stood between this well and the Guest-House. This was an auspicious discovery, because at that precise moment we were working in a room just opposite this very wall. I was literally standing on the other side of the wall from where the well would have been. You can see in map 3 there is also a little street that once led back to this well.

Whether it was fate, perseverance or luck guiding me through the maze of old maps, cobblestones and lost landmarks I will never know, but I am excited and proud to present the first possible school location that fits three of the four reference points. Since the

---

bonding arrangement of the brickwork at the lower level. The well was truncated at 6.99 m. O.D. and was recorded for a depth of 2.5 m. without being bottomed. The uppermost surviving part of the well was filled with a friable fine black (inorganic) silt, including moderate fragments of coal and a few fragments of clay pipe (153), representing a deliberate back-filling.

'Unfortunately, it was not possible to sample the tiles at the top of the lining, but two sampled bricks from lower down proved to be stock-moulded and belong to the post-medieval period. Adhering to them was a soft sandy mortar, quite different to that recorded at the top of the lining, and possibly dating to the sixteenth century. Either the bricks were re-used from another context, or the tile courses represent a rebuild above an earlier brick lining. The lining was not recorded in sufficient detail to make a decision either way. The fill marking the disuse of the well is provisionally dated to c.1680–1730.

'Its position, cutting the west wall of the Period IV.1 church, suggests that the well post-dated the demolition of its west front (and perhaps also the nave of the church). Unfortunately, the construction date of the well cannot be established due to the uncertainty as to whether or not its lining was composed of re-used material, while the demolition of the church's west front can only be dated to some time before c.1680–1730.'

Finding Saviolo's School

nineteenth century (and possibly earlier), historians and scholars have speculated on the location of Saviolo's school, but none has come so close to meeting all four Elizabethan descriptions. While I have been unable to find any trace or reference to a Red Lion sign hanging in this little street next to the recently rediscovered well, I have no doubt that someone may some day 'stumble across it'.

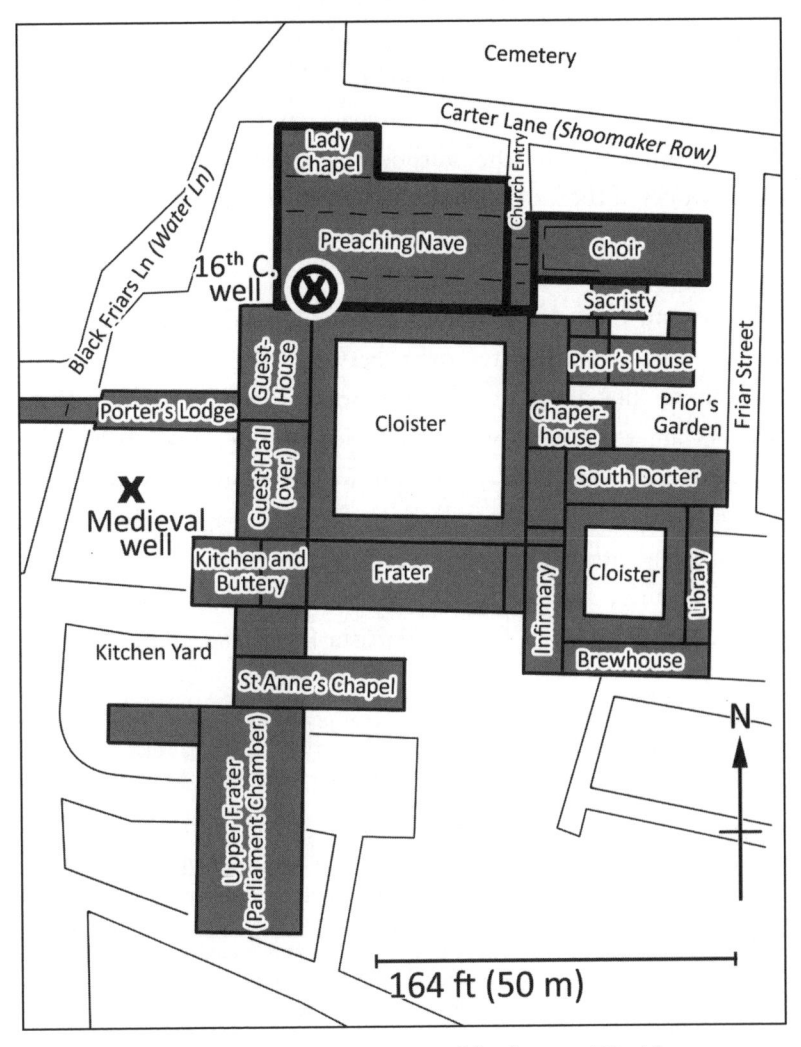

Map 4: *This is based on a reconstruction of the friary in Blackfriars.*

Saviolo the Author

The publication of fencing books and those concerning the codes and ethics of duelling were not uncommon in sixteenth-century Italy. There were dozens of gentlemen writing on these subjects, and a number of these books were republished numerous times. The most popular one on duelling codes was written by Girolamo Muzio in 1550.* His book took Europe by storm and was republished four times in two languages within just one decade. Muzio's influence on other authors was great, as was reflected in many works of the latter half of the sixteenth century including the work of Saviolo.†

Many scholars have incorrectly asserted that Saviolo's work is merely an English translation of Muzio's earlier duelling code. While several similarities exist between the two works, and sometimes they are in accord, it is not a direct translation. Both authors are expressing well-established and accepted behaviour concerning the *code duello*, but there are numerous parts that show Saviolo's work to be unique. Both books hold chapters that do not appear in the other. For example, Muzio, unlike Saviolo, discusses 'Of misdoings, and spells . . . ' When comparing other notable Italian authors such as Giovan Battista Pigna and another Italian

---

* Girolamo Muzio, *Il Duello del Mutio Iustinopolitano*, Vinegia, Gabriel Giolito de Ferrari e fratelli, 1550. Ruth Kelso, 'Saviolo and His Practise', *Modern Language Notes*, Vol. 39, No. 1 (Jan. 1924), pp. 33–5, although she wrongly attributes his first book to 1558.

† Kelso states: 'There is no mistaking the relationship. Saviolo borrows the whole *Of Honour & Honourable Quarrels*, the second part of *His Practise*, from Muzio's *Il Duello*, translating in large part literally, sometimes omitting, but adding nothing except a chapter deploring the fashion of secret combat, and at the end accounts of four famous quarrels and an unrelated discussion of the nobility of women.' An examination of both books shows many differences. The similarities are common to books of a shared subject matter and do not really support a statement such as: 'Saviolo borrows the whole *Of Honour & Honourable Quarrels . . .* from Muzio's *Il Duello*.'

fencing master, Achille Marozzo, comparable similarities and differences are found in their works when addressing the subject of the *code duello*. What makes Saviolo's work stand out from these earlier writers is that his is the first treatise of this nature to be published in English.

As we have seen, in 1595 Saviolo published his influential book, *His Practise in Two Books, The First Intreating of the Use of the Rapier and Dagger, The Second, Of Honour & Honourable Quarrels.* Some people have stated that John Florio was actually the author of Saviolo's book. This unsubstantiated claim is hard to believe due to the innovative system of swordplay discussed in the first part of the book.* Saviolo drew upon his broad travels and studies throughout Europe to create a refined approach to the use of the sword for self-defence. He claimed to have reduced the teachings of diverse masters and distilled five or six various systems of fence down to one unified one.

Saviolo never names his previous fencing masters, nor does he leave any hint as to where he may have trained away from his birth city of Padua. However his fencing method is one of reduction and refinement, which reflects the general Italian trend prevalent in the late sixteenth and early seventeenth centuries. He attempts to simplify fencing away from the complexity of guards and the emphasis on cutting actions found in earlier forms of European swordplay.

The first book, covering the use of the rapier and dagger, is presented as a dialogue between master and student, mimicking a much earlier tradition of educational grammar books or colloquia. The second part of Saviolo's treatise is a *code duello* addressing a popular subject of the time: honour and the duel. A *code duello* is literally a duelling code – any compilation of rules or laws related

---

* That said, it would not be surprising to find that John Florio assisted Saviolo in writing it. Florio's translation abilities were unparalleled in London at the time.

to the proper conduct and/or format of resolution concerning a personal quarrel through the use of arms. Saviolo's *code duello* became widely renowned with Englishmen of all classes and became a model for the proper method of seeking redress for honourable and personal conflicts.

This was not Saviolo's first published work though. His first one was never attributed to him. A publisher, Richard Jones, obtained a licence on 13 December 1589 for the publication of a book by Saviolo called *The Book of Honour*.[*] It was subsequently published by Jones in 1590 as a compilation called *The Book of Honour & Armes*, which is anonymous and commonly attributed to William Segar. Jones never claimed the work as his own. In the dedication of *The Book of Honour & Armes* to Sir Christopher Hatton, Jones wrote: 'take in acceptable wise the entent of the author', but left Saviolo's name out. This is clearly the book that Jones paid Saviolo for in 1589.[†]

I was curious as to why Saviolo would have published his first book anonymously and then a few years later include a similar book with his fencing treatise. By comparing *The Book of Honour & Armes* to *Of Honour & Honourable Quarrels* I found some clues. It is easy to see Saviolo's hand in the first book. Many of the chapter headings (and even some of the turns of phrase) are identical. At least 50 per cent of the chapter headings for the early book are the same as ones found in the laterbook (with many of the remaining ones being similar). Moving beyond the headings and looking more closely at the line details, I compared the first twenty-nine pages of *The Book of Honour & Armes,* which consisted of 782 lines, to *Of Honour & Honourable Quarrels*. Of those 782 lines, 548 were similar to lines found in *Of Honour & Honourable Quarrels*. In other words, 70 per cent of the original book can be found in *Of Honour & Honourable Quarrels*. Many authors at this

---

[*] Stephen Lee, p. 866.

[†] Ruth Kelso felt 'that for some reason Jones did not publish Saviolo's first book, licensed in 1589 . . .' but a cross-reference of the two books leaves little doubt.

time borrowed liberally from others, so it was necessary to delve further into the details of these 548 similar lines. In doing so I was amazed to find 27 per cent of the 'similar' lines are almost the same or identical.*

This does not hold true the other way around. *Of Honour & Honourable Quarrels* goes into much more detail than *The Book of Honour & Armes*. While we can never know exactly why he published another *code duello*, Saviolo's work of 1595 is most definitely an expanded version of the earlier one. It seems that he had much more to say on the subject in later years.

⋅→⇒◯⇐←⋅

Saviolo's End

How or when Saviolo died and where he is buried still remain unknown. It does seem that 1595 was a good year for him because: 'not only was his book published but, later that year, he married. His wife was one Elina Warner and, on the 12th of October 1595, they were wed in Westbury, Wiltshire.'†

In Silver's book of 1599 he simply states that '[Saviolo is dead],' so Saviolo could have died any time between the end of 1595 and 1599.

In an effort to find a more precise date I looked at the burial records for St Ann Blackfriars parish in London. While there are some very interesting entries, there is no record of Saviolo. The closest is a *'Vincensio molinere'*, who was buried 16 November

---

* In a cross-comparison of *The Book of Honour & Armes* with *Of Honour & Honourable Quarrels* twenty-nine of the first thirty-one pages were examined.

† Chatfield, 'Stranger 929'. Elina Warner is listed as marrying 'Vincensio Saviolla' in the Wiltshire records.

1599. This seems too late to be our Vincentio, as Silver's book was published in 1599 and must have been written even earlier. Neither the burial records in the state archive of Padua nor Wiltshire hold a record of Saviolo being interred around that time either.

⋅⟫⋅⟪⋅

Saviolo's Legacy

In his time in London Vincentio Saviolo had made a tremendous impact on the cultural scene. His books and style of fence were incorporated into many popular works of the time and by a variety of authors, most notably Shakespeare. It would have been difficult for Shakespeare not to have known about Saviolo, yet there is no evidence to support the idea that they ever met.[*] That said, Saviolo's influence on Shakespeare is unquestionable.

While the English nobility loved Italians, the lower classes typically did not share the sentiment.

> ... the cultural core of the land was still intensely parochial, matching the sturdy and simple-minded dislike of most things foreign among the ordinary people, who were as ever, ambivalent about these newcomers. Among the professional and learned classes, and particularly at court, Italy and the Italians were prized, for even if Rome was a dangerous haunt for Protestants, the glories

---

[*] It is also often speculated that Shakespeare learned Italian fencing. For example, Mary McElroy and Kent Cartwright stated: 'Actors earned degrees from fencing schools, and many frequented the one at Blackfriars, where Shakespeare is believed to have learnt the art of the fence,' 'Public Fencing Contests on the Elizabethan Stage', *Journal of Sport History*, Vol. 13, No. 3 (Winter 1986), p. 207.

of Northern Italy, particularly Padua and Venice, lured generations of Englishmen to scholarship and pleasure.*

The theatre reflected this Anglo-centrism with the villains or clowns often being foreign and using Italian terminology when fencing. This is crystal clear in the works of William Shakespeare, but as Joan Ozark Holmer points out, 'Shakespeare's drama, however, does not display the Italian jargon of fashionable fencing until after Saviolo's own work has appeared in print.'†

Shakespeare's *Love's Labour's Lost*, *Romeo and Juliet* and *As You Like It* are perfect examples. Shakespeare illustrates his knowledge of the *code duello* with characters like Touchstone in *As You Like It*, who pontificates about the manner and diversity of lies, and how a gentleman is or is not compelled to respond to the various degrees of lies. Orlando's duel with Charles also resembles one of Saviolo's stories.

Romeo and Juliet includes more Italian fencing terms than any other play in Shakespeare's canon – among them are the *passado*, *punto reverse* and *stoccata*. He also includes references to the Italian duelling code and the style of fencing at the time – all of which were included in Saviolo's treatise. For example:

> The description of Tybalt's swordplay in *Romeo and Juliet* is in line with the Italo/Spanish style of fencing that Saviolo describes in *His Practise*. And Shakespeare seems to ridicule the fantastic fencing terms of the Italians as well as poke fun at the boastful Rocco Bonetti with his allusion to Tybalt being the 'very butcher of a silk button.'‡

---

* Alan Haynes, 'Italian Immigrants to England, 1550–1603', *History Today*, Vol. 27 (August 1977), p. 534.
† Joan Ozark Holmer, 'Draw if You be Men', *Shakespeare Quarterly*, Vol. 45, No. 2 (1994), pp. 164–5.
‡ McCollum, p. 27.

A similar flourishing of this foreign jargon appears in the literary works of such Elizabethans as Thomas Lodge,[*] John Marston[†] and Ben Jonson,[‡] all of which postdate the publication of *Of Honour & Honourable Quarrels*.[§] By issuing this book containing foreign terms and etiquette, Saviolo gave English authors easy access to new source material, which they could easily adopt in their own works.

Saviolo's work was clearly known and read by many in his time. Revisiting *Of Honour & Honourable Quarrels* in the twenty-first century could prove to be as important to the English-speaking world today as the original publication was to sixteenth-century Londoners. The advice offered on public behaviour and maintenance of honour transcends the barriers of time. We may no longer defend ourselves with swords or hold honour in the high esteem earlier generations did, but our tempers, desires and egos are not so very different. Perhaps it is long overdue that we are reminded and re-influenced by the manners described in Saviolo's once popular book.

---

[*] 'This is a right malecontent Deuill . . . his Rapier punto r'enuerso,' in Thomas Lodge, 'Wits Miserie, and the Worlds Madnesse: Discouering the Deuils Incarnat of this Age', *The Complete Works of Thomas Lodge*, 4 vols, 1883; reprint New York, Russell & Russell, 1963, Vol. 4, p. 17.

[†] 'Oh come not within distance! Martius speaks, who ne're discourseth but of fencing feats, of *counter times, finctures*, sly *passatas, Stramazones*, resolute *stoccatas*, Of the quick change, with wiping *mandritta*, the *carricada*, with the *embrocate*. "Oh, by Jesu, sir!" methinks I hear him cry, "the honourable fencing mystery Who doth not honour? Then falls he in again, Jading our ears, and somewhat must be sain Of blades, and rapier-hilts, of surest guard, of Vincentio, and the Burgonian's ward",' A. H. Bullen (ed.), *The Works of John Marston*, Vol. III *The Scourge of Villainy*, London, Ballantyne Press, 1887, p. 373.

[‡] 'Cob. O, must you be stabb'd by a soldier? Mass, that's true! When was Bobadill here, your captain? that rogue, that foist, that fencing Burgullion? I'll tickle him, i'faith.' William Gifford, *The Works of Ben Jonson*, London, Warne & Routledge, 1860, p. 20.

[§] For a wide range of dramatic allusions to swordplay, see R. E. Morsberger, *Swordplay and the Elizabethan and Jacobean Stage*, Salzburg, Universität Salzburg, Institut für Englische Sprache und Literatur, 1974.

Part II

OF HONOUR & HONOURABLE *Quarrels*

The Second Book

LONDON
Printed by John Wolfe
1594

THE PREFACE

Forasmuch as diverse and sundry people have treated of the matter of single combats (whereof I have also framed this present discourse) and have not only grounded their opinions upon deep judgement and exact consideration of the subject they were to handle but also with all furniture of wit and words commended the same unto the view of the world, I might justly doubt (as being inwardly guilty of my own weakness and insufficiency) to go forward with the enterprise I have presently taken in hand. But my purpose herein is rather to discharge my duty and zeal to the nobility and gentry of England, by publishing this treatise to yield a testimony of my thankful mind for their manifold favours, than by froth of speech[*] to make my matter saleable or to purchase either credit to myself or acceptance of the reader. My hope is that such people to whose rank it belongs to manage Armes and to know the use of their weapon will no less favourably conceive of my endeavours and with their courtesies supply my defects. I have been ready by my painful and liberal diligence to deserve their likings and do now present my labours in the most humble degree of reverence.

---

[*] A speech that is an empty senseless show of wit or eloquence.

A DISCOURSE OF SINGLE COMBATS

WITH SOME NECESSARY

considerations of the causes

for which they are undertaken

When I enter into due examination of the first original ground and occasions of this kind of encounter and withal consider the corruption of man's nature through whose ambitious and insolent humours[*] these violent trials have been often practised, I cannot but allow the just complaints framed against man by philosophers and wise men of former times. By his industry and knowledge man is able to search out and attain unto the amplitude of the air, the hidden secrets of the earth and the revolutions of the heavens. Yet he is so disguised and masked in the judgement of himself, so reckless in his own affairs, that he never

---

[*] Saviolo is here referring to the theory of physiology, in which the state of health and state of mind are governed by four elemental fluids. These fluids are blood, yellow bile, phlegm and black bile; they are called sanguine, choleric, phlegmatic and melancholic, respectively. It is important to keep all four humours in balance. It was common to characterise a person by their humours.

effectually considers of his own proper nature and inclination, much less endeavours to reform what by the eye of reason he might find controllable and blameworthy in his disordered affections. If as every man is by nature capable of reason and understanding, so he would dispose and order the conveigh* of his life, so he might be reported no evil speaker, no liar, no deceiver, no quarreller, no traitor to his friend or injurious to his neighbour. Those who have written of this subject might well have spared their labour, and this rigorous kind of congress had been either not known at all or much less practised than it is. But since it is a thing common in experience, and usually seen, that through want of government in some persons (who giving themselves to the full current of their disposition, making their will their God and their hand their law) matters are carried in a contrary course, it is necessary that something be written of this action, even as much as shall be consonant to reason and judgement, at least to limit and restrain the manner of proceeding in quarrels, if not utterly to remove the occasion of unnecessary strifes and fruitless contentions. Otherwise instead of order we should follow confusion and deprive both our own actions and all things else of their due and just ends.

The premises considered it is no marvel if diverse persons, giving themselves wholly to the bent of their own indiscretion and want of judgement, esteem of things clean contrary to their nature and quality. For if a man frames himself to lead a civil and temperate course of life, some will say he is a fool. If he is not quarrelsome, he is a coward. If no gamester, he is of base education. If no blasphemer, he is a hypocrite. If neither whoremonger nor bawd, he is neither man nor courteous, but altogether ignorant of the rules of humanity and good fellowship. A lamentable state is that where men are so misled by ignorance and self-love as thus to over-smooth and colour their vices and imperfections with the names

---

* The management, conduct or path of his life.

of virtues and to think any action current* that is done by them, and authorised by their irresistible sway and distempered appetites.

What has become of the gentility and inbred courtesy of ancient noble gentlemen? Where is the magnanimity of the honourable knights of earlier times, whose virtues as they are recorded in histories wherein we read of them, so ought to have been left to their posterity, that in them we might see the image (now forgotten) of ancient true nobility? Since all things fall to decay, it is no marvel though that virtue (I speak with all due reverence and favour) is found but in a few. For surely there are many in whom nothing remains but the bare title of nobility, in that they are gentlemen born. In their manners they wholly degenerate from their ancestors and make no account either of honour or dishonour, giving themselves to such pleasures as their unbridled appetite leads them unto. Neither can I ascribe any reason to this their sliding from virtue to vice, contrary to the course taken by their honourable ancestors, but this – that whereas while their fathers lived their bringing up was committed to tutors of good government and discretion, their parents being dead they withdrew themselves from their virtuous kind of life, leaving and rejecting the sage counsels of their instructors and cleaving to their own devices. If they amend not and take a better course, such gentlemen will lighten shame and destruction.

Wherefore, by way of advice, I wish all men to avoid evil company. For the most part this is the cause of great and infinite loss of honour and life as well as of goods and possessions. They should instead follow virtue, bearing themselves with a sweet and courteous carriage towards every man. By this course they shall gain commendation and credit and shall be esteemed of all men, and, avoiding all such occasions of dislike as may be offered, obtain a good and honourable reputation. Does not God forbid a private

---

* In this context 'current' mean generally accepted or prevalent at the moment.

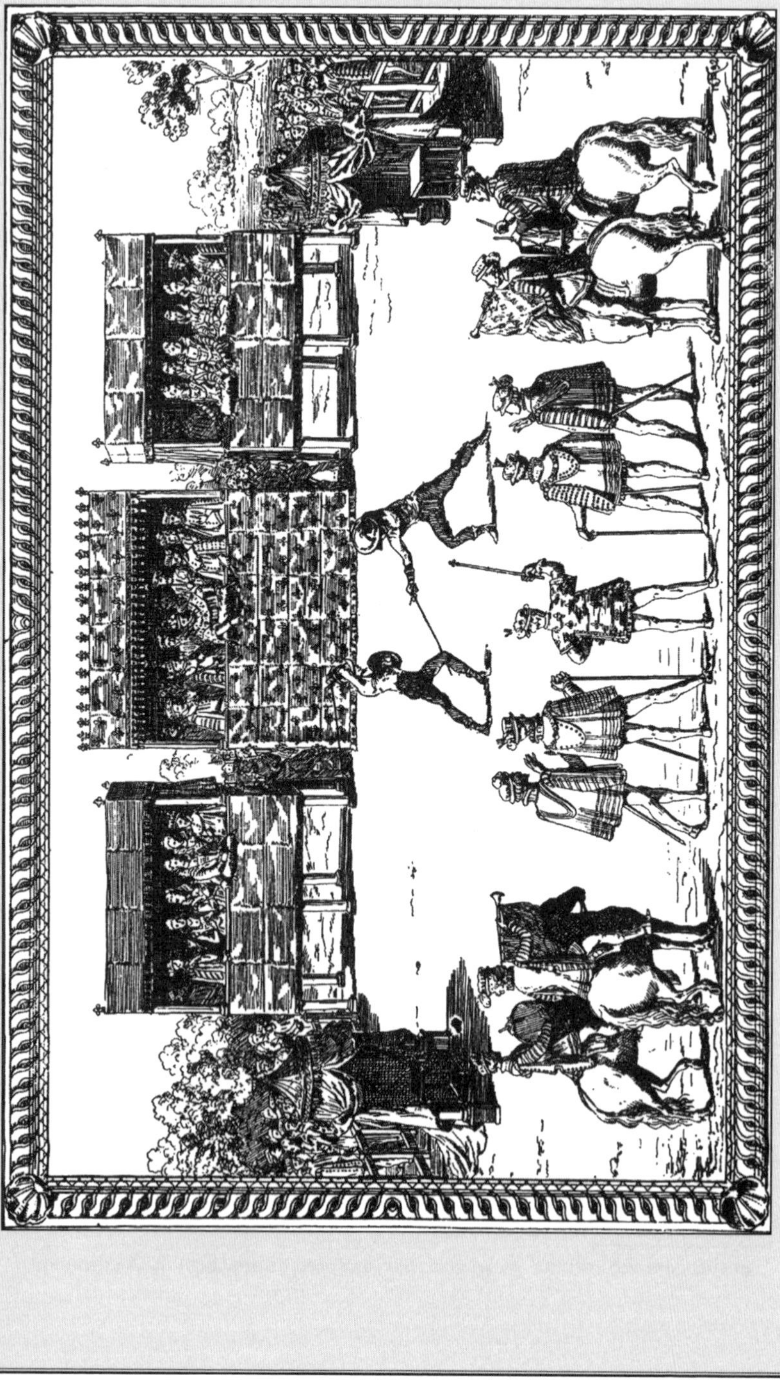

Duel between Jarnac and Chateigneraie

This nineteenth-century engraving depicts what is arguably one of the most famous 'duels' in history. Taking place in France on 19 July 1547, during the reign of Henri II, this formal combat is unique in that it is considered by duelling historians as the last of the formal 'chivalric duels' or 'trial by combat'. The encounter between the aggrieved parties took place on a 'champ clos' (closed field) in a preselected and designated area.

This formal combat between Guy Chabot Comte de Jarnac (Jarnac) and François de Vivonne, Seigneur de Chateigneraie (Chateigneraie), who were both kinsmen and neighbours, resulted from an accusation that Jarnac was being 'kept' by his father's second wife. Chateigneraie held to the position that Jarnac told him that he had a liaison with his stepmother. Jarnac, upon hearing of this accusation, gave Chateigneraie 'the lie', meaning that Chateigneraie was a liar. Jarnac demanded that his honour be restored, and Chateigneraie accepted the challenge, requesting a 'field' from the king. Francis I granted the request, but then withdrew it. Upon the death of Francis I, Chateigneraie petitioned King Henri II for a field, and his request was granted. The sovereign decided that the combat would take place in thirty days, both gentlemen having a month in which to prepare for the ordeal. Chateigneraie was an experienced warrior and was renowned as a man at arms. On the other hand Jarnac was ten years younger and inexperienced. He therefore enlisted the services of an Italian fencing master.

On the appointed day, after all of the formalities and ceremony were completed, the men entered the field. Upon the signal to commence, they quickly advanced and met each other, giving and receiving many blows and several inconsequential wounds. Jarnac, adhering to his fencing master's teachings, executed a high feint at Chateigneraie's head. As Chateigneraie raised his buckler to defend, Jarnac passed his blade under the defending shield and gave a cut to the ham of Chateigneraie's left leg behind the knee. Jarnac pursued the attack and followed with an immediate cut to the ham of the right leg. From that moment this technique became known as the coup de Jarnac.

Chateigneraie fell but vainly attempted to continue the combat, only to be disarmed. Jarnac, not wishing to take advantage and desiring not to kill his adversary, pleaded with Henri II several times for a decision. However the king did not utter a word. After repeated pleading, the king was advised to have Chateigneraie's wounds attended to, but Chateigneraie, feeling utterly disgraced, refused treatment and died from the loss of blood.

man to kill his neighbour? It is manifested in sacred scriptures against Cain to whom God said that the blood of Abel his brother cried from the earth for vengeance against him,* showing thereby that he abhors murder and will revenge it in due time.

Moreover, he created us naked without anything naturally given with which to offend or hurt,† whereas other creatures have some of them horns, other claws, others strong and sharp teeth and others poison. Thus we were created of almighty God, to the end we might live in peace and brotherly concord as the sons of God, not as the children of the Devil. They are the inventors who discovered the use of weapons to offend their neighbours and maintain the authority of their father the Devil, who was a murderer from the beginning and takes pleasure in the destruction of men, raising dissention between families, cities, provinces and kingdoms. Upon such occasion, the necessary use of Armes has got such credit in the world.

Kings and princes have nobilitated some with the name of knights for their excellency therein, which name is made noble and that upon great reason. For such men as have purchased nobility by conquering kingdoms for their princes, more respecting their honour and country's good than any other thing and esteeming less

---

* A likely version that Saviolo would have read says: 'And the Lorde said vnto Cain: where is Habel thy brother? Which sayde I wote not: Am I my brothers keper? And he sayde: What hast thou done? the voyce of thy brothers blood cryeth vnto me out of the grounde. And nowe art thou cursed from the earth, which hath opened her mouth to receaue thy brothers blood from thy hande.' Genesis 4:9–11, The Bishop's Bible, 1568.

† A likely version that Saviolo would have read says: 'God saide: "Let vs make man in our image, after our lykenesse, and let them have rule of the fisshe of the sea, & of the foule of the ayre, and of cattell, & of all the earth, and of euery creepyng thyng that creepeth vpon the earth." So God created man in his owne image, in the image of God created he him, male and female created he them. And God blessed them, and God sayde vnto them: be fruitefull, & multiplie, and replenishe the earth, & subdue it, and haue dominion of the fisshe of the sea, and foule of the ayre, & of euery lyuing thing that moueth vpon the earth.' Genesis 1:26–28, The Bishop's Bible, 1568.

of life than of death in regard to preserving that honour unblotted, which belongs to knights, ought not in any wise to be destitute of high reward.

In so much that Armes being doubled by so many valorous men, it would be a great shame for one of noble of spring not to be able to speak of Armes and to discourse of the causes of combats, not to know how to discern the nature and quality of words and accidents, which induce men to challenges, not to be acquainted with the manner of sending cartels[*] and challenges, and how fitly to answer the same. In a word, not to have so much experience in these affairs as to accord the parties challenging and challenged, bringing them from their hostile threats to loving embracements and of quarrelling foes to become loving friends, all causes of discontent being taken away on either side. The ignorance whereof has in these times bred great mischief, for many think that an injury being offered in deed or word[†] the matter may not with their credits be taken up before they have fought, not regarding if they be injured indeed. They ought first to examine what he is who has done it and upon what occasion he might do it. If in word, what quality the person is who spoke injuriously and whether he deserve an answer or no. For a man being carried away with choler[‡] or wine may chance to utter that which (his fury being passed) he will be willing to make any satisfaction – wherefore it were fondly done by him that would fight upon every word. Neither can I be induced

---

[*] 'Cart['e]l: [m.] a challenge, a cartell, a defiance, a libell.' Richard Perceval, *A Dictionarie in Spanish and English, first Published into the English Tongue by Ric. Percivale Gent, 1591. Now Enlarged and Amplified . . . by John Minsheu*, London, Edm. Bollifant, 1599. 'Cartello: a cartell, a chalenge, a defiance, a libell.' John Florio, *A Worlde of Wordes, or Most Copious, and Exact Dictionarie in Italian and English, Collected by John Florio*, London, Edw. Blount, 1598. For details see 'Of the Form of Cartels, or Letters of Defiance' on p. 89.

[†] See 'A Rule and Order Concerning the Challenger and Defender', on p 66. Saviolo also discusses the satisfaction of each on p. 67

[‡] Choler is one of the four humours (see footnote on p. 39). One who is choleric has a ready disposition to violence and is easily upset.

are most convenient ornaments whereby men shall avoid many dangers and quarrels.

There are also certain indiscreet men whose gross fault I cannot overslip without blaming. These men, as they either stand or go in streets, stare and look men passing by them in the face as if they would for some reason mark them. This breeds such an offence unto some men so marked that they cannot take it in good part, and therefore it is very dangerous. It may happen that a man may look so upon one who either is by nature suspicious or by reason of some secret thing known to himself may suspect that he is therefore looked upon. Whereupon great quarrels may arise, for the man so looked on may fall a questioning with him that looks on him, who perhaps answering him crossly may both move him to choler and be moved himself also, and so bring the matter to some dangerous point. I have myself seen a notable example of this: passing through the city of Trieste in the uttermost part of the territories of Fruili in Italy I saw two brethren, one a most honourable captain and the other a brave and worthy soldier, who walking together in the streets were very steadfastly eyed by certain young gentlemen of the city. They stared the captain and his brother in the face something unseemly and (as they took it) discourteously, whereupon they asked the gentlemen in very courteous manner whether they had seen them in any place before or whether they knew them. They answered: 'No'. Then replied the captain and his brother: 'Why then do you look so much upon us?' They answered, because they had eyes. 'That (said the other) is the crows' fault, in that they have not picked them out.' To be short, in the end one word added on the other, and one speech following the other, the matter came from saying to doing. What the tongue had uttered the hand would maintain. A hot fight being commenced it could not be ended before the captain's brother was slain and two of the gentlemen hurt. One escaped with the rest, but the chiefest cutter of them all was hurt in the leg and so could not get away. He was taken, imprisoned and shortly after beheaded. He was very well beloved in the city, yet he could not escape this end being brought by following his mad-brained conceits and being misled by evil company. The rest of his company was banished from their country. Now if these gentlemen had more courteously and wisely demeaned themselves, no more hurt would have followed that bad beginning. Every man therefore shall do well to have a great regard in this respect, lest like disorders be to their danger committed.

Furthermore I do not like the custom that some men have in meddling with other men's weapons, especially with those that profess Armes. Neither can I think it over-wise for men to be viewing one another's rapiers, because this inconvenience may arise: a man may thus take occasion to kill his enemy towards whom in outward appearance he carries himself as his very friend (for all is not gold that glisters). You may think a man to be your friend whose heart is hid from your eyes, so also is unknown unto you all the mischief which may be avoided by discretion and foresight in offering no occasion or opportunity for the effecting thereof.

Moreover when men light into the company of honourable gentlemen they ought to have a great regard of their tongue, to the end they say nothing that may be evil taken or misconstrued. In talking or reasoning to gird* at any man, or find fault with him, howbeit you may do it never so truly, for it is ill playing so as it may prick and it is not good jesting to the disgrace of another.

It is no less behoveful for men to beware that they do not entice or suborn other men's servants, which of itself is odious and purchases naught but shame and reproach to the performers of such base practices.

I must also dislike those who offer wrong to other men's servants, for besides betraying their baseness of mind they seem also to resemble him of whom the proverb says, being unable to

---

* To jeer, mock or taunt.

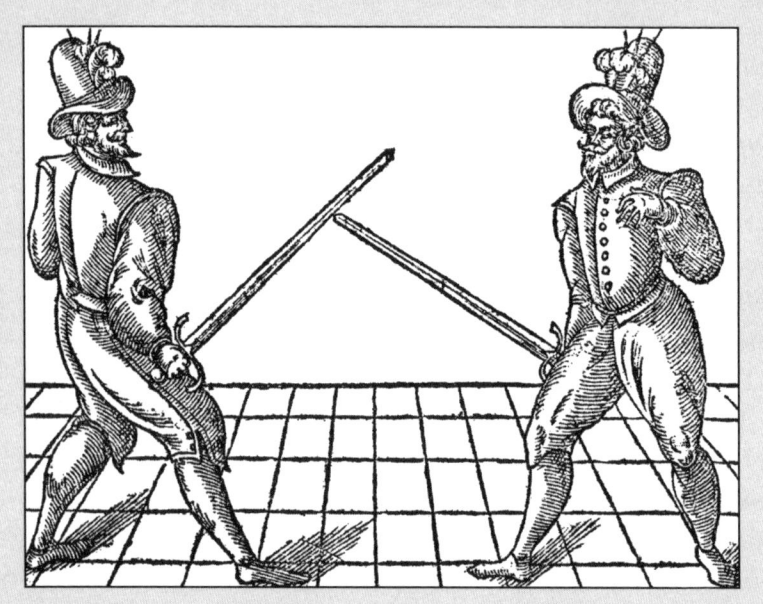

Above: *Vincentio Saviolo illustrating a guard with the rapier.*

Below: *Vincentio Saviolo illustrating his rapier and dagger.*

strike the horse, beats the saddle. This signifies as much as when he is not able to deal with the master he wreaks it on the servant. I hope therefore that gentlemen will consider how base a thing it is to do this and also how often much hurt ensues. For one house is by this means stirred up against another, and whole families are turned upside down. For whosoever sees his servants abused will think himself wronged and will therefore endeavour to revenge such wrongs, as offered unto himself. According to the proverb, love me and love my dog.

Also gentlemen ought to abhor carrying of tales and reporting of other men's speeches, for that is a very unchristianly action unworthy to proceed from a brave and free-minded man. For such as use tale-bearing often thinking to report but words, report that which causes a man's destruction. On the other side, if any man chance to speak evil of you in your absence you should not seek a means to be revenged of him who so does, despising and condemning him. For a common saying it has been of old times (be it spoken with reverence) he that speaks of me behind my back speaks with that which is behind my back. Sure it is that no man of value or virtue will speak anything of a man in his absence but rather to his face. Neither must a man easily give credit to all things which he hears. For whatever he is who carries tales does not, nor cannot, truly deliver a man's speech wholly without addition or subtraction. A word or two is easily adjoined, which not withstanding is effectively sufficient to alter the whole state of the speech. This may move any man to think it a vain matter to go about to maintain any quarrel upon no better grounds. It may fall out that, by giving credit to tales, one may endanger himself and his friends. Every man shall therefore do well to bridle his own tongue and to consider other men's speeches before he credit them and not report unto his friend everything he hears spoken of him, unless it concern his life or reputation. In such a case a man ought to warn his friend to the end he may be provided against the wrong which is intended against him. In this case I also wish this observation to be kept, that the party grieved first goes to him who spoke the words and ask him in a courteous manner (not without courage) whether he has reported or spoken such words, etc. If he denies this in the presence of credible person, then he who reported it is to be charged with the injury. If he acquits himself by proving that which he reported to be true, yet considering that the party accused has denied them before witness, you are to rest satisfied and contented for by denying them he recalls them.

Furthermore let every man take heed that he does not maintain any dishonoured or infamous person's quarrel of whatever condition or calling he is.

It is also wisdom for a mean man[*] not to deal with men of great calling. For he shall be sure howsoever the matter goes to get little by it. If chance, some occasion of quarrel being offered, he let it slip suffering the matter to be taken up, he shall do well to retire into some place further off. It is better for men to live as friends asunder than as enemies together, when every small matter which might happen would renew the old quarrel. Hence comes it that this proverb was used; that the eye sees not, the heart grieves not.

Contrarily a man of great calling and authority should not to wrong any man of the meaner sort. There are many who, howbeit they are but poor and no authority, yet they want neither valour nor courage and will rather die than take any injury. I will explain two or three examples which I have seen myself.

There is a certain village about a mile from the famous city of Padua in Italy where the Boggiarini dwelt, men well to live for their calling wanting neither heart nor courage. As it is a custom throughout all Lombardy in summertime there are many places

---

[*] A man of limited means; humble, poor or lowly. 'I Holde housholde as a meane or poore man dothe . . .' John Palsgrave, *Lesclaircissement de la Langue Francoyse*, London, Johan Haukyns, 1530.

A Discourse of Single Combats

in castles and villages where great markets and wakes[*] be kept. Upon the days of such saints as the parish churches are dedicated unto, resort merchants and countrymen of all sorts, from places far and near, make merry and good cheer having good country music. After dinner and supper the younger sort use all exercise and pastime, dancing with their loves on a fair green kept for the purpose. To this dancing diverse gentlemen would resort, only to see the countrymen and women sporting and using their rural pastimes. Among these gentlemen were two nephews to the duke, who spying two maidens among the country wenches surpassing all the rest in beauty and comeliness, being sisters to the Boggiarini, fell into such liking of them that within some few days they went unto the house of the said Boggiarini accompanied with certain gallant youths, thinking by gifts and fair smoothing speech to persuade and entice the maidens to become their paramours and follow them home to their places. The maidens' father and two of their brethren came to the gentlemen, having had an inkling of their intent, and told them that they were very poor and not able to entertain them according to their calling, yet that notwithstanding such was their honesty that they greatly regarded their reputation, wherefore if it pleased the gentlemen to come to their house with honest intent they would stretch their power to the uttermost to pleasure them and their gratefulness of mind towards them for their courtesy in vouchsafing to come unto them. If they came on any other intent than virtuous then they beseeched them to depart. Hereupon the maddened youths who accompanied the gentlemen began to draw upon the countrymen, who being far less in number than the gentlemen were forced to retire and save themselves in their house, and for that time the matter was so ended.

Not long after, the Boggiarini chanced to meet some of these gallants where two of the gentlemen were shrewdly handled. For

---

[*] A traditional festival held in commemoration of the church's patron saint.

this cause the two Boggiarini were committed to close prison by the magistrates and remained so for the space of eleven or twelve months, and then were released. The gentlemen, understanding that they should be released, departed suddenly the next day from Venice with seven lusty fellows well armed intending to kill the Boggiarini and so went to Padua. On the other side, the Boggiarini's kinsmen being informed of their cousins' release out of prison hastened to Padua to bring them home and carried them their weapons.

Therefore having discharged all duties after they were set at liberty they took their journey in hand and went homeward. The gentlemen meeting them at a place called Seruy rushed violently upon them on the sudden, all crying with a loud voice, 'kill, kill, kill'. They did not know what they meant at first, but quickly after perceived who they were, would not willingly have had to do with them as by oaths and protestations they declared, defending themselves as well as they could and retiring back to escape them. Being compassed around and seeing no way to escape death but by the death of those who assailed them, they perceived that neither entreaty nor protestation nor anything could move the revengeful gentlemen to hold their hands, even after so many injuries before that by them offered as having gone about to violate their sisters, having beaten their father and having obtained punishment for themselves by the magistrates with a year's imprisonment.

Being content with nothing but their lives, at length after they had retired much and sought all means to avoid the fight, they began to set apart all respects, abandoning their lives. Laying on with all their strength and no less courage, in short space they slew the duke's nephews both and another gentleman, and hurt diverse others who accompanied them. Only one of the Boggiarini was harmed with the loss of three fingers. The fight being ended, one of the Boggiarini getting on a miller's horse escaped, the other three

A Discourse of Single Combats

– purposing to save themselves in a monastery – were taken and put in prison.

Afterward, their cause being brought before the Council of Venice, an uncle of the gentlemen who were slain undertook the patronage and defence of the poor countrymen (they being in truth guiltless) and making a speech for them obtained so much that their lives were saved, howbeit they were banished out of all the territories of the Venetian seignory.* The end of these gentlemen who were so pitifully slain may be an example to all others how to behave themselves towards men of meaner† degree.

In the same city of Padua happened another cause not much unlike this between a gentleman of Brescia‡ and a baker. This gentleman, having many houses in that city (in one of which the baker was tenant), upon some small occasion gave the baker warning to find himself another house. The baker being an honest man got all his neighbours to entreat the gentleman to let him continue his tenancy but their entreaty served not and the poor man to his utter undoing was thrust out of his house. This so grieved him that he vowed his landlord's death, who, having had some notice thereof, took heed as best he could, continually coming home before night, lest by his late being abroad he might be endangered. Thus two years having passed he began to wax more careless little and little thinking in that space a man might forget any wrong. The poor baker had not so forgotten that great injury, for I have heard many say that the offender writes in the sand, but

---

* 'Seignory' is the power or authority of a feudal lord, the territory over which a lord holds jurisdiction. See 'Seigniory (Fr.) a Lordship, or the jurisdiction of a Lord', in Thomas Blount, *Glossographia Anglicana Nova: Or, A Dictionary, Interpreting Such Hard Words of Whatever Language, as are at Present Used in the English Tongue, with Their Etymologies, Definition, &c. Also the Terms of Divinity, Law, Physick, Mathematicks, History, Agriculture, Logick, Metaphysicks, Grammar, Poetry, Musick, Heraldry, Architecture, Painting, War, and All Other Arts and Sciences are Herein Explain'd . . .*, London, D. Brown, 1707.

† See footnote on p. 52.

‡ Northern Italy in east Lombardy, east-north-east of Milan.

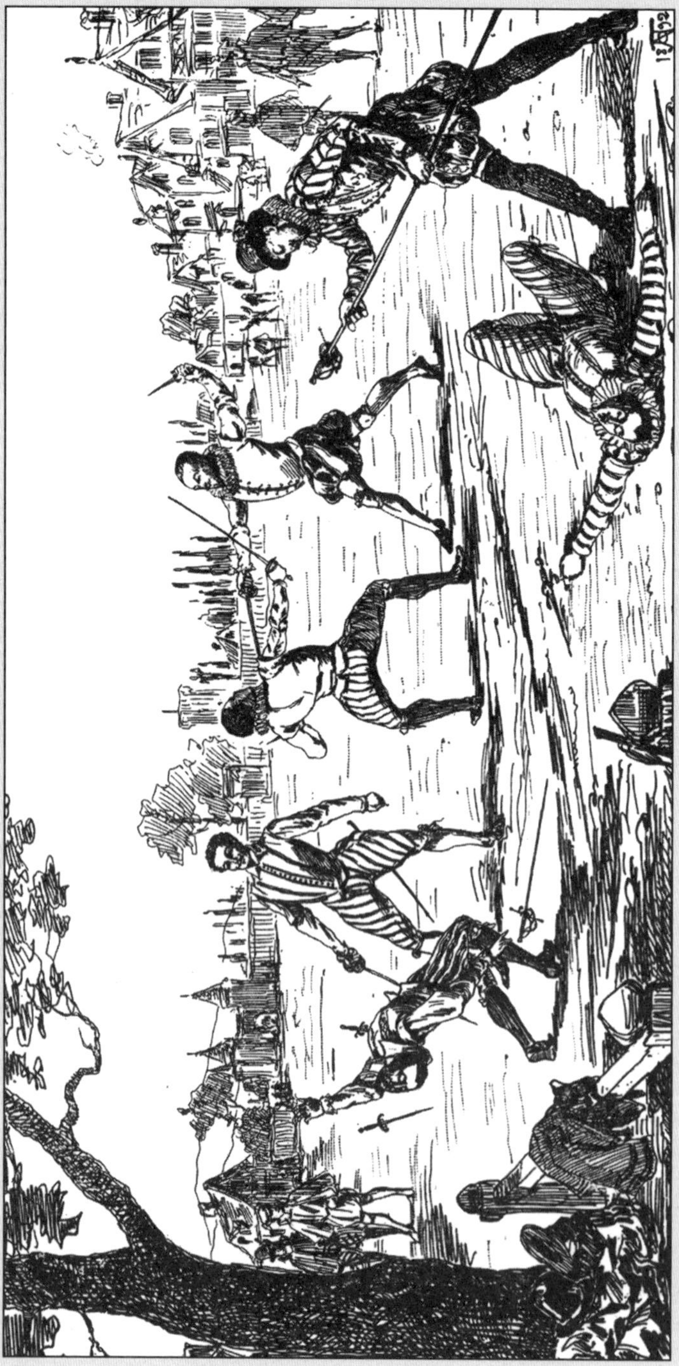

Duel des mignons

This nineteenth-century engraving depicts one of the most famous duels in French history. Taking place on 27 April 1578 during the reign of Henri III and known as the Duel des mignons, it was one of the instances where the savage nature inherent in armed combat manifested itself within the context of a duel.

Mignon is a term meaning a favourite of the king. In this case two of Henri III's mignons – Quelus and d'Entraguet – developed an animosity towards each other over their amorous interest in a lady. Maugiron and Livarot seconded Quelus, while his selected assistants Riberac and Schomberg seconded d'Entraguet. During this era it was the custom in an affair of honour for the seconds to join in the combat along with the two principals.

In the furious rush of the combatants, the seconds – Riberac and Maugiron – died of sword thrusts through the body. The other pair of seconds engaged with each other, and Schomberg severely opened up the cheek of Livarot with a horrible cut. The latter, however, ran Schomberg through the chest and killed him instantly.

The principals – Quelus and Entraguet – engaged with vigour, the former armed with a rapier and the latter with a rapier and dagger. In the first exchange Entraguet received a slight thrust to the arm and the hand of Quelus was severely mangled. As the fight progressed, Entraguet, in making use of the rapier and dagger, stabbed his adversary several times in the body, and Quelus fell from exhaustion and loss of blood. On falling, Quelus asked Entraguet to be satisfied, and the combat stopped.

Some weeks later Quelus – the king's favourite – died of his wounds. Henri III was so angered and stricken with grief that he forbade all duelling in his realm on pain of death.

the offended in marble. So this baker meeting the gentleman late in the night hastily runs into a shop where cheese and such like things were sold, where borrowing a knife makes after his old landlord and overtaking him, cuts his throat. The gentleman within few hours died, and the baker was banished by the magistrates because they could not otherwise punish him, he being fled.

I have read in the history of the last wars in Persia how Mahomet Bassa,* general of the Turkish empire, took a certain pension from a soldier (who for his valour had well deserved it) and bestowed it on some other whom he thought better of. Whereupon the soldier, being with great reason offended, feigned himself mad and the better to effect his purpose seemed to think that he had entered into some order of Mahometan religion.† He came into Bassa's chamber daily mumbling out his prayers, where Bassa and all the rest about him laughed. The soldier did this often until he espied a suitable opportunity and slew Bassa. Being taken and brought before the great Turk,‡ he was given to Bassa's slaves to do their pleasure with him for he had confessed the whole matter unto the Turk.

Before the overthrow of the Turkish navy, which was in the year 1571,§ the States of Venice had sent Sforcia Palanisino, their general, a little earlier into Slavonia by land and into other eastern parts with that authority as in time of wars generals used to have.

---

* An old spelling for Sokullu Mehmet Pasha (1505–79), who was Grand Vizier under Suleyman I (1520–66) and Selim II (1566–74). Towards the end of his reign Suleyman gave control to Mehmet, a model followed by Selim II when he took the throne.

† An old spelling for Mohammedan, the Christian term for Islam at this time. For example: Robert Carr (trans.), *The Mahumetane or Turkish Historie Containing Three Bookes: 1 Of the Originall and Beginning of the Turkes, and of the Foure Empires Which are Issued and Proceded Out of the Superstitious Sect of Mahumet . . .*, London, printed by Thomas Este, 1600.

‡ Sultan Suleyman the Magnificent (1494–1566).

§ Don John of Austria, commanding the fleet of the Holy League, defeated the Ottoman Turks in the waters at the mouth of the Gulf of Patros.

He, having arrived in those places, espied an opportunity to take a certain city called Margarita. He levied an army with all speed and marching towards the city planted his ordinance and began to batter the walls. At the assault he bare in his hand a kind of pickaxe, with a thing like a hammer at one end and a long pike at the staff end, able to pierce anybody armed with a curats.[*] This kind of weapon is much used by the Slavonians, Croatians, Turks, Albanians and Hungarians. With this pickaxe Sforcia Palavicino encouraged his soldiers to strike those who returned from the assault or were not so forward as they ought to have been. Among others a certain Venetian gentleman would have been stricken, but his servant presently stepped before his master to Sforcia with his piece[†] in his hand and bade him hold his hand for he whom he was about to strike was a gentleman of Venice and his master, and therefore willed Sforcia to take heed of touching him, purposing, if Sforcia had not retired from his master, to shoot him. Sforcia noting and admiring the fellow's valour and fidelity in hazarding his own life to save his master from wrong earnestly requested the gentleman to let that servant be his, promising to show him much favour. The gentleman, both to gratify Sforcia and to advance his man to preferment, did. Sforcia made him a captain and wonderfully enriched him insomuch that in a few years he became a great man.

It is a gross folly for men to scoff and jest at others in whatsoever case it is. Neither should those men who by nature are framed comely and tall to be girding at those whom nature has not been so beneficial. There are many who being carried away with plausible conceit of their own manhood and strength, by reason of the properness and greatness of their well-shaped bodies, despise men

---

[*] A common sixteenth/seventeenth-century spelling of 'cuirass'. A cuirass is a piece of armour for protecting the breast and back, yet sometimes referring to the breastplate alone. See George Cameron Stone, *A Glossary of the Construction, Decoration and Use of Arms and Armor: In All Countries and in All Times*, New York, Jack Brussell, 1961.

[†] A gun.

of less stature, thinking in respect of themselves they are nothing. If occasion were offered to fight with them, they think they would be able to mince them as small as pie meat, not knowing that men are not measured as woollen cloth by the yard or that little men have often overthrown great fellows. In consideration whereof I will recount unto you what happened in Italy in the city of Bologna.

When the Emperor Charles V[*] came to be crowned by Pope Clement VII, this emperor had in his train a great Moor like a giant, who beside his tallness wanted no valour and courage, being wonderful strong. He, enjoying the favour of so great an emperor, was respected of all men and particularly of diverse princes who accompanied the emperor. This brought him to such a proud conceit of himself and his own worthiness (ascribing the good favour of all the princes and gentlemen who followed the emperor to his own deserts, and not to the good will that they saw the emperor bare him) that he laughed all men to scorn, thinking none able to encounter with him.

He then obtained leave of the emperor that a proclamation should be made. If anyone in that entire city, being so full of people, would wrestle with him he would challenge him. This being published every man was sorely afraid of his hugeness, strength and eager countenance. None could be found who dare undertake the match, except for the Duke of Mantua's[†] brother, Rodomont, who though he was of an ordinary stature yet he was both very strong and nimble withal and (as it was credibly thought) all his breast was wholly made of one bone. He was very valiant and by report could break seven staves tied together at one course. Insomuch if he had not had a good horse he should break his back except for many rash enterprises he was banished from all tilt-yards and justing.[‡]

---

[*] Charles V was crowned by Pope Clement V on 24 February 1530.

[†] Federico Gonzaga was the Duke of Mantua 1519–40.

[‡] Tournaments. 'Tournement [(Fr.)] a turning, rounding, revolution [a cor]; [trans.] a converting, changing, exchanging, translating, a bending or inclining

A Discourse of Single Combats

Rodomont seeing that no man else dare undertake to be matched in wrestling with the proud boasting Moor, notwithstanding that his brother the duke and the rest of his kindred used all means to dissuade him, would nevertheless wrestle with him to make it known unto all the world that he would not suffer so beastly a creature to stain the honour of Italian gentlemen and give the emperor (who was a stranger) occasion to laugh at the Italians, seeing them put down by a monstrous Moor. Rodomont therefore buckling* with the Moor in presence of the emperor and all the princes behaved himself in such sort that the Moor could not foil him with any fall. Eventually he was brought only to touch the ground with one knee, although the Moor strained himself to the uttermost strength. The night drawing on, after they had tried their force a long time the emperor caused them to cease till next day. At this time Rodomont came to meet the Moor again with great courage. Having now had good trial of his strength and knowing what he was able to do, as soon as he saw fit opportunity he nimbly took the Moor about the middle and clasped him hard against his own breast, holding him thus until he perceived him to be breathless. Letting him slip out of his arms the Moor fell down dead so heavily that the whole place shook as if some steeple had been cast down. Rodomont perceiving this presently got away from the whole company. Taking a post horse he fled, fearing lest the emperor should have done him some displeasure, but the emperor went not about it, considering that the challenge was publicly proclaimed by his own leave and authority, howbeit he was grieved for the loss of his stout Moor.

One more example will I recount concerning insolency, especially because the Rodomont of whom I spoke was an actor in the tragedy. It happened that the Duke of Mantua and his

---

towards. It was in Queen Elizabeths dayes an exercise in great request among our nobility, called also justing or tilting, & c.' Blount, *Glossographia*.

* Grappling, seizing or taking hold of.

brother Rodomont, being in the same Emperor Charles' court about certain affairs of their own, walked into a great chamber expecting the emperor should send for them when his majesty was at leisure. Into this chamber at the same time came a certain Spanish captain, who, without any greeting or salvation, came by them and bravely walked between the duke and his brother, nothing respecting the greatness of that prince and so braved them three or four times. Wherewith Rodomont, being greatly offended with the discourtesy of this proud and insolent captain, went to a window which he perceived to be open and, staying till the captain came that way, took him by the collar with one hand and putting the other under his breech thrust him out the window and broke his neck. Whereupon he fled from the court with all the speed he could. But the emperor being informed of the matter blamed not Rodomont, considering the Spanish captain had so insolently behaved himself to Rodomont's brother, the Duke of Mantua. It is an endless thing for me to rehearse all the examples I have heard concerning this vice of insolency. These are infinite and happen daily in all countries by reason of the little regard had in the bringing up of young men. I will only exhort every man to take heed lest himself fall into like folly.

 I will not omit to speak of a certain vice and part not to be used by a gentleman, seeing it proceeds of mere cowardice. This is when a man, having fallen out with one or other and wanting courage to deal with him in single fight, procures base and cowardly means by the help of some of his friends, with whom he plots how they may circumvent his enemy. And so watching him, at some time or other will draw upon him as if he had met him by chance, who thinking upon no villainy, without any suspicion at all, likewise draws to defend himself, as a man ought to do. This is when the other plotters standing afar off do draw near as strangers to them both and unwilling any hurt should be done on either side. They most traitorously will either themselves impart a thrust by the way, or so strike his weapon that his enemy may take occasion to hurt him.

This villainy (for I think no term bad enough to express it by) you may escape if you take heed when anyone draws upon you that none come near you, willing them to retire, with protestation that you will take them as your enemies if they do not. By reason that you do not know them, they cannot but like of your protestation, if they mean you no evil, seeing that you can not assure yourself of their good affection towards you and care of your safeguard. Therefore in any case, at such time as you shall happen to be enforced to defend yourself suddenly, let no man come near you for it is very dangerous. I speak this because I have seen the like done very often and found it confirmed by great experience.

To say something of parting, I will by the way declare thus much. He who will part two who are fighting must go between them both, having great regard that he neither hinders one more than the other, nor suffers the one more to endanger his enemy than the other. If more than one comes to part, they must divide themselves and some come on one side, some on the other, taking great heed that neither of them are in any way either prejudiced or favoured. Wherefore I do not disagree with the great Duke of Florence's opinion, who upon pain of great forfeiture forbade all men to part those who should fight. He would have those suffered to fight till they parted themselves, and if any one chanced to be hurt they should blame themselves, seeing they were the only cause thereof.

If the like were used in all places, I think we should see half the quarrelling daily among gentlemen. For surely many will be very ready upon no occasion to draw upon a man, only because he knows that he shall not be suffered to fight.

There are some others who to wreak themselves upon their enemies will do it by a third means – by gifts or promises, persuading some needy fellow to pick a quarrel with their enemy. Either the poor fellow hurts or kills him and so incurs danger of death or at least is hurt and maimed himself. Therefore I could wish every man to meddle only in his own quarrels, neither revenging his own wrong by another, nor wreaking other men's injuries by himself, unless he have good reason to the contrary, as in diverse cases a man may honestly and honourably both entreat others to revenge his wrongs and also be entreated of others.

There are also some gentlemen so careless that being in the company of honest gentlemen think that whatever folly they commit the company will be ready to defend them. They will either scoff or gibe with those who pass by, or use some knavish trick towards someone who is not of their company, or fall a quarrelling with one or other whom they think good. Having set many together by the ears they are the first who will run away or hide themselves in some corner till all is done. By my counsel therefore no man shall be so fond as to back any, or take part with any, who are so void of discretion or government.

Similar to these you shall see others who will invite their friends to some dinner or pastime abroad only to serve their turns in revenging their wrongs, having plotted a means for the execution thereof. Many times much harm has been done, sufficient to cause any man to beware of falling into like inconveniences.

All which I have here said, I have had experience of myself. These are the things whereof quarrels proceed. These beginning, but between two or three, sometime are so far increased that whole families are wrapped in quarrels and broils which often are not ended without great hurt and bloodshed. Every man should therefore know how to behave himself in these cases and not presume upon his own skill or knowledge, but learn how he ought to proceed in matters of combats or quarrels. For a man may daily learn more than he knows, and especially they that want experience: seeing it is a matter seldom seen, that he shall be able to know what is good, that has not had some trial of that which is evil. According to a verse of Petrarch: 'Every one must learn to his cost."* This saying pertains especially to young men who for the most part can never learn to govern themselves aright until such time as they have had experience of some or other mishap concerning their goods, life or credit. As nothing is so dangerous but may be prevented, so in this point – that men take good heed and arm themselves with the sure shield of sound counsel and advice so that they may easily avoid such errors, as I have discovered and now make known for their profit and commodity.

This is a discourse most necessary for all gentlemen who have in regard their honours touching the giving and receiving of the lie. Whereupon the Duello† and the combats in diverse sorts ensue, and many other inconveniences for lack only of the true knowledge of honour and the contrary, and the right understanding of words which here is plainly set down beginning thus.

---

* Francesco Petrarch (1304–74). From *Il Canzoniere*, poem 105, verses 31–3.
'*Proverbio "ama chi t'ama" è fatto antico.*
I' so ben quel ch'io dico: or lass'andare,
ché conven ch'altri impare a le sue spese.'
('An ancient proverb is "Love who loves you."
I know well what I say: now I grow weary,
For it is necessary that others learn at their own cost.')

† 'A single combat, a fight betweene two.' Florio, *A Worlde of Wordes*.

A RULE AND ORDER
CONCERNING
THE CHALLENGER
and Defender

All injuries are reduced to two kinds, and are either by words or deeds. In the first, he who offers the injury ought to be the Challenger. In the later, he who is injured. For example, Caius says to Seius that he is a traitor, unto which Seius answers by giving the lie. Thus ensues that the charge of the combat falls on Caius, because he is to maintain what he said and therefore to challenge Seius. Now when an injury is offered by deed, then they proceed in this manner. Caius strikes Seius, gives him a box on the ear or some other way hurts him by some violent means. Wherewith Seius, offended, says unto Caius that he has used violence towards him, or that he has dealt injuriously with him, or that he has abused him or some such manner of saying. Whereunto Caius answers: 'You lie'. Whereby Seius is forced to challenge Caius and compel him to

A Rule and Order Concerning the Challenger and Defender

fight to maintain the injury which he had offered him. The sum of all therefore in these cases of honour is that he unto whom the lie is wrongfully given ought to challenge him who offers that dishonour and by the sword prove himself no liar.

There are many who delighting to find fault with that which is set down by others, be it never so truly and exactly performed, will in this case also seek to overthrow the rules which I have above alleged concerning challenging and defending. They oppose many arguments and objections which I think frivolous to trouble the reader withal. Therefore will I neither recite them here, nor spend so much labour in vain as to answer them. Men but of mean* capacity will be able to discern and judge of the small reason that they are grounded upon. For who is there who sees not, howbeit some men finer witted than endowed with valour and courage, will by multiplication of speeches give cause of greater offence and thereby give the other occasion to challenge the combat rather than to do it themselves. Yet that notwithstanding, the true and perfect manner of proceeding in cases of honour is that whosoever offers injury by deed, as striking, beating or otherwise hurting any man, should presently without any further debate or questioning be challenged to the combat, unless he refuse the same by making satisfaction for the offence or offered injury.

In injuries offered by word, no respect ought to be had of all the words which answers and replies are multiplied by (as when one says 'You lie', the other answers with the same words, and the first replies with 'You lie also', and so may perchance make a fray with words only. This foolish and childish manner of proceeding cannot but be disliked by gentlemen of reputation). To whomsoever the lie is unjustly and wrongfully given, unto him shall it belong to become Challenger and by Armes maintain what he spoke or did whereupon the lie was given him.

---

* See footnote on p. 52.

Of Honour & Honourable Quarrels

WHAT THE REASON IS THAT THE PARTY UNTO WHOM THE LIE IS GIVEN OUGHT TO BECOME CHALLENGER AND OF THE NATURE OF LIES

Some men marvel why he unto whom the lie is given ought rather to challenge the combat than he who is called a traitor or a villain or by some other injurious name. It would seem more reasonable that he who is most injured should become Challenger and not the other, and that it is a greater injury to say unto a man: 'You are a thief' or 'You are a villain and a traitor' than this: 'You lie'. But the laws have no regard of the words or of the force or efficacy of them, but provide that the burden of the challenge shall ever fall on him who offers the injury.

It is thought that every man is honest, just and honourable until the contrary be proved. Therefore as in common trial by civil judgement and order of law, whoever is accused of any crime is delivered from condemnation by simply denying the same, unless further proof is brought against him. Even so in this case: whoever speaks of another man contrary unto that which is ordinarily presumed of him, it is great reason that the charge of proof should lie upon him to make that manifest unto the world by force of Armes that such a man is guilty of such and such things as he has laid to his charge. Hereupon some may cavil and ask how he who is injured by deed shall become Challenger (as I have said) if the laws provide that the burden thereof shall belong unto him who offers the injury.

Whereunto I answer that if I beat or strike any man thereof proceeds no cause of proof. It is manifest that I offend or hurt him and I know no cause why I should prove that I do so. But if the other says unto me, that I did not as a gentleman worthy to bear Armes, or that I dealt not honourably or any such thing, I repel his sayings with the lie, and force him to maintain what he has

A Rule and Order Concerning the Challenger and Defender

spoken. Whereof I am acquitted with sole denial* till he makes further proof.

Now, concerning the nature of lies, I say that every denial, be it never so simple, bears the force of a lie being altogether as much in effect. I see no other difference between a simple denial and the lie than is between a speech more or less courteous. Wherefore although the names of denial are diverse as: 'You lie', 'You say untruly', 'You speak falsely', 'You spare the truth', 'You tell tales', 'You regard not how falsely you report a matter', 'You are wide from the truth', 'This is a lie, a tale, a falsehood', etc. Yet all these manners of speech import the lie, whether he unto whom they were spoken spoke injuriously or not. For though I do not say any evil thing of any other, but chance to discourse of some matter, or recite some tale or history or report anything as occasion of speech may be offered me, if someone who stands by tells me I say not truly, or use any of the foresaid forms or manner of speech unto me, surely he brings my truth in question and causes me to be reputed for a liar, and consequently offers me injury.

Forasmuch as every injury offered by words may be the first time wrested† and returned upon him who offers the injury, I may lawfully repulse that injury with a second denial which shall bear the force of a lie. Whereby his first shall be accounted of the nature of an injury by which means the burden of the challenge shall rest wholly upon him. But if he chance to say only thus, or after this manner unto me: 'This is not so', or 'the truth hereof I take to be otherwise', etc. I cannot take any such speech injuriously. It may be the thing whereof I spoke is not true, and yet I do not lie. Therefore such a speech so spoken cannot in any ways burden me, unless I shall make some injurious reply thereunto which he, repealing with the lie, may lay the burden of challenge on me.

---

* The denial is giving the lie or any variation of denying what injurious thing a man has said of you.

† Turned around, twisted or bent.

A word comes sometimes to be injurious and sometimes not, only by being sometimes injuriously spoken and sometimes not. For example, if one man says unto another: 'You say not true', he does thereby make him a liar and so he does injury him. But if he do reply and say in this manner, 'that which you say is not so', or 'it is not true', etc., then no such manner of speech or saying can be injurious. As I have mentioned above, the thing may be false and yet he is no liar, by reason that he either may be ill informed, or not understand the matter as it was or some such other thing might happen, whereby he might be moved to report and speak that again which is not true. Wherefore any such answer whatsoever cannot in any sort fall burdenous unto him.

One exception is if he say that he did such a thing, or that he did say such a thing, or that he had been about such a matter, or that he dealt in such a case, etc. and if another answers him that he did not, or that the same which he said was not true, etc. For so he is burdened being accounted a liar, because a man cannot be misinformed in anything which he said or did himself. He is to repulse this injury with the lie so the charge of challenge remains on the other. Unless he is saying that he did or said such or such a thing and do thereby offer some man injury, who by giving the lie may repulse the same injury and so cast the charge of challenge upon him. To conclude, by all this which is said it manifestly appears that whosoever takes heed that he offers no offence in his words or speech shall never be endangered to be injured with the lie.

OF THE MANNER AND DIVERSITY OF LIES

To the end that the nature of lies may more easily be known and when the lie ought to be given, when not, and in what cases, it is

A Rule and Order Concerning the Challenger and Defender

requisite I should particularly discourse thereof. For some lies be certain and some conditional. In both the first and the later some of them are general and some of them special. Unto these two sorts, I will add a third kind of lies, which may be termed vain lies.

OF LIES CERTAIN

Lies certain are such as are given upon words spoken affirmatively. For example, if any man should say or write unto another: 'You have spoken to my discredit and in prejudice of my honour and reputation and therefore do lie.' In this respect this is a lie certain, because I affirm that such a one has spoken evil of me. Yet, because I do not particularly mention wherein or how he has offended me by speech, the lie I have given him is general and therefore of no force. To have the lie given lawfully it is requisite that the cause whereupon it is given be particularly specified and declared. Wherefore lies special, and such as are given upon sure and express words, assuredly bind the parties unto whom they are given to prove the same which they have spoken. They cannot deny that they have said whereupon the lie was given them. For example: 'Alexander you have said that I being employed by his highness in his service at Pavia have had secret conference with the enemy, wherefore I say that you have lied'. This is a sure and a specially and by consequence lawfully given.

OF CONDITIONAL LIES

Conditional lies are such as are given conditionally. For example, if a man should say or write these words: 'If you have said that I have offered my lord abuse, you lie or if you say so hereafter, you shall lie. And as often as you have or shall so say, so oft do I and will I say that you do lie.' Of these kind of lies, given in this manner, often arise much contention in words and diverse intricate worthy battles, multiplying words upon words whereof no sure conclusion can arise. The reason is because no lie can be effectual or lawful before the condition is declared to be true, that is, before it be justified that such words were certainly spoken. The party unto whom such a lie is given may answer accordingly whether he finds himself guilty or not. If by chance he has said so, he may by general words seek means to escape the lie which is given him. And withal upon those words which the other has spoken or written to him he may happily find occasion of a mere quarrel and give him a lie certain. On the other side, if indeed he has not spoken those words whereupon the lie was given him, then may he say absolutely that he spoke them not, adding thereto some certain or conditional lie. For example: 'Whereas you charge me that I should say that you are a traitor and thereupon says that I lie I answer that I never spoke such words and therefore say that whosoever says that I have spoken such words, he lies.' Yet notwithstanding I cannot like of this manner of proceeding because thereby men fall into a world of words.

Some hold an opinion that such an answer might be framed: 'You do not proceed in this case like a gentleman, neither according to the honourable custom of knights. When you shall do, I will answer you.' Unto whom I cannot give applause considering the other may reply that he lies because he says he did not as a gentleman, etc. alleging that many gentlemen have observed and

A Rule and Order Concerning the Challenger and Defender

used that manner of proceeding. The other shall have occasion by his ignorance, in not knowing how to answer the lie conditionally given him, to give him a certain lie. Therefore, not to fall into any error, all such as have any regard of their honour or credit should by all means possible shun all conditional lies, never giving any except certain lies. In like manner they ought to have great regard that they do not give them unless they are by some sure means infallibly assured that they give them rightly, to the end that the parties unto whom they be given may be forced without further 'Ifs' and 'Ands' either to deny or justify that which they have spoken.

OF THE LIE IN GENERAL

The lie in general is considered in two sorts: the one having respect to the person, and the other to the injury. That which touches the person is termed 'general' when no especial person is named to whom the same is given. As if one should say: 'whosoever has reported of me that I have betrayed my lord does lie falsely.' To this lie it is held of brave men of reverence that no man is bound to answer the same. This seems to me to be excellent well understood because this charge or imposition may seem to touch many, being that many have spoken the same, and so one with many should be bound to fight. This is to grant an inconvenience directly for it is not allowed that any man should enter into combat more than once for one quarrel, and that no man shall put his honour upon another man's sword or valour. So might it come to pass that such a one might take the quarrel that the lie was never meant for. Whereupon, to avoid such disorders, the best mean is that this lie so given is not adjudged lawful, nor approved for sufficient.

Of Honour & Honourable Quarrels

The other lie, which we have termed general in respect of the injury, is this: 'Antony you have spoke ill of me, or you have said somewhat in prejudice of my reputation, and therefore I say that you have lied.' This lie, for it is upon words in which the lie especially, did not declare what the thing is from whence the slander was or prejudicial speech to reputation spoken is. In many sorts a man may be ill spoken of and one's reputation prejudiced. It happens very often that he who talks of another man in diverse matters speaks that which he of whom they were spoken might esteem to his shame and disgrace. Therefore it is most necessary to express the point whereupon he holds himself offended. To the end that it may be considered whether he will take upon him to prove his sayings or whether he will prove it with his weapon, or civilly by the law. Thus for these causes this lie cannot be accepted in no ways of value nor lawful. He who has given the same, if he will come to the definition or determination of quarrel, must write the particular and declare it for in right he is bound to do so, if so much time is permitted.

And this I say, a lie given in this sort does not only bind but is very dangerous to be wrested. The danger whereof I speak is thus, as by this case following you may easily see.

Paul understands that Nicholas has said of him that he is a usurer,[*] and having understanding of these words writes unto him: 'Nicholas you have spoken ill of me, and therefore I say you lie.' Paul peradventure,[†] knowing many more defaults than this in Nicholas, may be answered thus: 'I confess that I have spoken ill of you, but I specified the particularity of that which you have done.' I said that long since you committed such a fault, and such another, and show

---

[*] One who lends money and charges an excessive rate of interest, which was considered a sin. 'In thee have they taken gifts to shed blood; thou hast taken usury and increase, and thou hast greedily gained of thy neighbors by extortion, and hast forgotten me, saith the Lord God.' Ezekiel 22:12.

[†] Perchance, perhaps, possibly.

A Rule and Order Concerning the Challenger and Defender

how and thus bring forth the ground of his speech without making mention at all of that particularity which Paul charged him with. This he may add more: 'you lie yourself saying that I speaking ill of you do lie'. Here, if Paul returns to write he should reply: 'I say that you lie in saying that I am a usurer.' Not for all this shall his lie make him guilty, because the general lie permitting an exception it may be well wrested, being apparent that, in speaking ill of Paul, Nicholas did not lie. After the first lie is accepted false it is to be presumed that also the second contains a kind of falsity. Whosoever is accounted naught once is always esteemed naught in the same kind. The presumption being against Paul, it behoves him to be the actor so as for the effect in the generality of the lie he shall fall into this inconvenience. Besides, such may be his default as the same by law might be proved against him, that neither as defendant nor plaintiff he may enter the Duello or combat. I conclude therefore, for the small validity of the general lie, that it has the quality to put another man to the pains of proof. All cavaliers[*] and brave men ought to take heed of the danger it brings altogether. Although there were no other thing than to avoid the multitude of cartels,[†] a thing is more comely for gentlemen to bind themselves to the action than lay themselves open with many words.

OF THE LIE IN PARTICULAR

The special lies are those that are given to special persons and upon express and particular matter. The example is this: 'Silvano you have said that at the day of the battle of St Quintin I did abandon

---

[*] Men of gentle birth, i.e. aristocrats.
[†] See footnote on p.45.

the ensign, whereof I say you lie.' This is a lie that we termed before assured and lawful. It is very necessary that he who goes to work thus must have such proofs and witness of the speech that he which intends to begin the repulse with the lie, that the other may not deny it. If I do not have proofs convenient he may answer that I have lied myself in giving him the lie. In such a case I shall not only be driven to prove that I did not abandon the ensign but prove that he has laid that blame upon me unjustly. If he cannot justly deny it then there is no doubt that he must also prove it.

When he shall deny he spoke these words and I have proved them by just circumstance, if then he asks for the combat to prove his saying that way then the same is to be utterly refused. The denial of his speech comes to be an unsaying of his word. Thereupon it is to be presumed he was a liar as well in his accusation as denial. In these quarrels wherein appears manifest falsity those who command (as sovereign lords) should not to permit the combat, nor brave men (I mean cavaliers) should not be ashamed in such cases to refuse the battle. It is more honourable to avoid it with reason than to enter it against all right and all bond of duty.

We would in this chapter specify that only brave men ought to give the repulse unto all injuries incurred by this true and lawful lie. When they find themselves offended by anybody and will either by mouth or writing give it, they must so perfectly manifest themselves in the words wherein they find themselves outraged, and in such sort build their intent so that not one of their words may be denied nor wrested so they do not determine afterwards to have question or doubt of the Challenger or the Accused, which is in English the plaintiff and defendant.

A Rule and Order Concerning the Challenger and Defender

OF FOOLISH LIES

The common opinion is that he who gives the lie loses the election of weapons,* so that he say unto another that he lies without having regard to the manner how he does it. This way he thinks to have done great matter. Hereupon it comes that every day there rises new and strange foolishnesses from the common sort. For example, he who will give the lie before the other speaks saying: 'If you say that I am not an honest man you lie in your throat.' This is a changing of nature. The lie being but an answer, in this manner it comes to answer that which was never spoken.

Here let us put a case. It is true that sometimes one hearing that another has said he is a thief will answer: 'If you say that I am a thief you lie.' This lie is general, held incontinently to charge another. But the form of this gives (as it seems unto me) means and way for the speaker thereof to resolve with himself well whether he will continue therein or no. As though he would say to himself, take heed if you will affirm that which you have spoken, that avouching it I pretend to give you the lie. If he does not return to say the same then that lie does not bind. A man may sometime repent himself, saying something in choler or with little consideration.

Now to return to our foolish lies, whose fashion will give cause of laughter: 'If you will say that I am not your equal, you lie.' He does not only answer himself before the other has spoken, but also puts himself upon his pleasure. Say what I can, till I have spoken it I do not lie. I cannot say that I am going to France, until I am on the way and I have embarked.

Of such similar lies I have heard some good stories among no common men. There are not any of these more right than this which is much used: 'In that you have spoken ill of me you lie, and if you deny the same you lie also that if I have spoken ill of you, or if

---

* The defendant chooses the weapons to be used in the duel.

Seeing now mention is made of writing to him who far off speaks ill of another I will add this. I know that it is said of some that whoever is the first to write is accounted Challenger. This opinion is in no sort to be allowed, for the Challenger is he who moves the quarrel. He offers the quarrel who gives the injury, whether it is by word or deed present or far off. For the other shall not prejudice the matter with the manner of writing, the writing first or last is no matter at all. I have seen it disputed among the wisest sort of gentlemen that cartels of dementy, or giving the lie, being here and there cast abroad, everyone did defend for themselves to be the first who published, pretending among themselves that he who was the first to write would have the best advantage.

Supersticery is not only considered in respect of the advantage of weapons or of persons, but also for respect of privileged places or the sight of the prince (where it is not lawful for one to freely show his grief). Here one may ask me what he should do if in the presence of the prince one will give him outrageous words. To this I will always thus answer: that neither should he let pass the repulse by the lie nor the prince ought at all to take it in disdain. For he ought rather to be tolerated who gives another a repulse of an injury than he who does it.

He who bears that in his presence an injury should be done me, of a greater reason ought to bear that I defend the same, but yet so, and with such reverence, he must answer the same by adventure as the same may seem full of modesty. This I will now say, that so much the more I hold myself bound to answer by how much I know he did me injury is accounted of the prince before whom I may be accused.

Herein I prescribe no law to anybody, but only show mine opinion. Whosoever follows it shall do honourably and for his reputation. Whom shall not like to follow it, let custom stand instead of law. And now turn to say that princes should more patiently comport the discharge than the charge that another has given in his presence.

A CONCLUSION TOUCHING THE CHALLENGER AND THE DEFENDER,

AND OF THE WRESTING AND RETURNING BACK

of the Lie, or Dementy

I come to the end of this treatise of dementies, or giving the lie, and conclude the question of the Challenger and the Defendant. We have already determined that he to whom the lie is given for repulse of an injury is properly the Defendant. To the end that more clear contentment may be given we are very diligently to examine the lawful dementies, or lies. By this examination remind ourselves (if it be convenient) of those things that we have treated before, their manner and principally the proper nature of the lie, which is to put back the injury. When it does not this office

A Conclusion Touching the Challenger and the Defender

it becomes an injury itself and with another lie the same may be repelled. Upon this consideration I say that the lie may be given in the affirmative and so upon the negative. Sometime it falls out that upon the affirmative it cannot be given and sometime upon the negative it has no place. Consequently both here and there being given it may be wrested and sent back. Yet it may be given both in the affirmation and negation in the same quarrel without that it may be subject to any repulse of either of the parties.

Here I will give an example of each of my opinions. The lie lawfully given upon the affirmative is such as before we have set down in more than one manner. One says of another that he is a rebel unto his lord, he who answers says that he lies. This lie cannot be avoided, being that it is given in the repulse of the slander which is laid upon him. But if I should say of any man that he were an honest man and one should give me the lie upon these words, in this it requires no repulse but is an injury. I may say that he should lie who thinks that I should lie. Now it is his part to prove that he is not an honest man, as well by reason I gave him cause of injury. It is presumed of every one that he is honest if the contrary cannot be apparently proved. Whosoever says that another is unhonest must prove the fault committed for which he ought not be esteemed an honest man.

Now let us pass over to the lies which are given upon the negative, whether they are lawful, or lawfully may be turned back or no. For example; if one should say of me that in some matter of Armes or fighting I did not do my duty and I should answer him with the lie, the same shall be a most lawful answer. For in that speech that I had not done my duty he puts on my back no small burden of infamy. It shall be most lawful and convenient that I should discharge myself with the lie, here the repulse of an injury being the lie. The presumption is in my favour. A man must not presume of another but that he does his duty in all respects. Whosoever goes about to give me that blame, to him it appertains to be esteemed Challenger. If one says that he has not failed in his loyalty to his lord and I should answer him that he lies, he may say unto me, you lie in that you say I lie. With great reason it may be said. Having answered me so, he is not doing injury unto anybody with those words, nor should any man presume that another should be disloyal. With the lie which I give him I do not defend myself nor any other of any injury, but go about to outrage him. He may lawfully return back that lie and I come directly to be dementied, so consequently must become Challenger.

Now it rests that we show unto you the examples of these cases in which every and the self same quarrel, both upon the affirmation and negation you may give the lie, so that neither of the one side nor the other is there any means, or way, left to give them the repulse. It is thus.

Two gentlemen or cavaliers are brought to the steccata[*] to fight. There are weapons presented unto them upon. They reason and debate between themselves whether they are refused or not so long that the day is passed without coming to the battle or fight. There does arise a question hereupon among them whether they be refused or no.

This man, whosoever he is, says that with reason they might be refused and does charge him who brought them. He says that they may not be refused in reason and charges him who refuses to fight with them. Therefore the task being given as well on the affirmative as negative the lie may accordingly be given and no more the affirmative than the negative may it be wrested, or sent back, being both in the one and in the other manner given for repulse and not of any injury. Thus much may suffice to be spoken of this subject, seeing that the other manner of lies, how they should be given and which may be wrested and which not, thereby appears that they are fully demonstrated which are lawful.

---

[*] 'Steccato: the listes or place to combat in, or other place railed in with stake, railes or poles. Also a combat.' Florio, *A Worlde of Wordes*.

A Conclusion Touching the Challenger and the Defender

Those known, it follows consequently to know who ought to be accounted Challenger. And so (God be thanked) we find that we have almost dispatched this matter, no less uneasy (as it is said before) to be handled and understood than necessary to be known of all cavaliers and gentlemen.

⋄⟶⟵⋄

OF INJURIES REWARDED, OR DOUBLED

Here yet there rests a new question, yea, even in the Challenger and Defendant, which we will not let pass without some declaration. This is in such cases when on the one part they speak and on the other they answer with injurious words. Either they reply the same, or do adjoin unto them others, so I now address requited injuries, or redoubled.

Requited injuries I understand as when one replies only to the injury that was given him, and adjoins nothing thereunto. For example: 'you are a thief, a thief you are'. The redoubled I call those when one is not contented to have said to his adversary the self-same words of outrage, but does join thereto another or more. For example, if I should say to another that he is a false moneymaker, and he should say to me I am so, and a homicide also. Upon these causes the writers of Duello move many questions, whether upon them there should be any fighting or not. If they should fight, which should be Challenger and which the Defendant? Herein to show you that which I think, before I speak anything at all thereof, I do adjudge him an ill-brought-up gentleman who feels himself to be charged with any blot of infamy and shall not be as well attentive to take that away, as to seek with like or greater injury to slander his adversary. He ought to put back that which was spoken to him with a lie, rather than reply the same or multiply any other in words. In doing so two commodities will follow him. The one, that with the lie he shall charge his enemy with that duty to be Challenger. The other is that he shall make himself known a person far from injurious intention. If the case happen in any of the forms aforesaid, there is somewhat to be marked how a man must behave himself therein. Therefore I say when one calls me traitor, and I say you are a traitor and do not thereto only join any word that has not the force of the lie, no combat is to follow. If he comes to reply the same injury many other times, it shall be as much as if an injury was once repulsed. There is no more repulse to be spoken of.

But if it should be answered: 'You lie that says I am a traitor for you are the traitor', I do not see wherefore the combat should not follow here. With these words I have discharged myself with he who charged me and laid upon him the slander of traitor. I send back the injury done to me and injure him with the repulse thereof, binding him to his proof. Although he should reply: 'But you lie yourself that I am the traitor', for all this he is not discharged but answered to that injury I gave him. Because the lie was given of me in time it will have the greater reason and is required at his hand to prove the truth of his speech. If, having called me traitor, I should answer him: 'You are the traitor', and he afterward subjoins 'You lie', now the case of Challenger will come upon me because he does not stay himself upon the first injury but answers to that which I said to him. Now to me there remains no more means to bind him to the proof, being made Challenger already with the lie given me. Neither can it be said that the answer – 'You are the traitor' – has the force of a repulse so much as that of an injury. The repulse stands in the negative, and if the negative has not the force of a lie it charges not. Being answered traitor, the injury with a lie may be put back lawfully. Although it is true, an injury once wrested will not permit any more writing.

It is to be understood that there is great difference between the wresting and repulse. With the wresting, I say to you that which

A Conclusion Touching the Challenger and the Defender

you say of me. With the repulse I give you not that blame you give me. I only free myself thereof, charging you with no blame at all, just with the duty to prove what you have said and that which I say should be so. If one should say that I am a thief and I should answer him that he lies, this shall be termed injury, and not wrested but repelled. If to one of these lies which we have showed before, which have the nature of an injury, an answer should be made to them by another lie, this shall be called wresting. This is a true resolution, and so it is approved and followed according to the style and order of gentlemen and cavaliers. And that which I have said of rewarded injuries, I say the same of the redoubled. He must not be termed Challenger by the multiplication of injury, but must be ruled by the lie I have said to you before that about question of words, the proof of the laws are appointed to the injurer and not to the injured. True it is that when neither of the one side nor the other the lie is, he shall not remain without some blame to whom the same was first spoken, how many or great so ever they are.

Nor is that to be taken for good advice which is set down by some writers, that if I should call another traitor, and he should answer that I am a traitor, a thief, a robber by the highway, I should subjoin that I will prove to you with my weapon that I am neither traitor, thief, nor robber by the highway, but that you are the traitor yourself. What a foolish enterprise shall this be of mine. Having the means to make myself Defendant, I will make myself Challenger and offer myself to the proof. Besides, what an ill kind of proceeding should mine be, to come to the determining of so many quarrels with one battle or combat, the same not being granted for diverse things together. It may come to pass in the one they may be true, in the other false; and so fight for the one with reason and the other without. Those who will form quarrels ought to be well advised that if they are not framed correctly, the lord, before he gives licence for the field, must reform them, or at least provide that when the gentlemen or cavaliers are conducted to the field that their godfathers* in capitulation give them a convenient form.

⋄⇌◯⇋⋄

THAT STRAIGHTWAY UPON THE LIE,
YOU MUST NOT TAKE ARMES

In the discourse about the lies we have concluded that the lied (which is he who has the lie given to him) is to be Challenger. We do not say that that presently a man should run to his weapon. For the trial of the sword being doubtful and the civil certain, the civil is that way by which every man of reckoning and reputation ought to justify himself. He ought to be esteemed most honourable who with certain proof approves his honour, than the other who does think to answer his reputation with an uncertain testimony. I see among notable gentlemen such an abuse that they think themselves to have committed villainy if they attempt any other means than by the sword. Wherein how much those who think so deceive themselves I will say nothing else at this moment but that the civil proof is the proof of reason and fighting just the proof of force. Reason is proper unto man, and force of wild beasts. Leaving the civil proof and taking the Armes, we leave that which is convenient for men to have recourse to that which belongs to brute beasts. Peradventure, gentlemen would not do this very often if they understood their duty well. They would well consider that it is no less the part of a cavalier to know when well to put up his sword than well to draw it out.

Therefore those who think they have the lie duly given them, if they have means by the way of reason to prove their saying, ought

---

* 'A Padrino: Padr['i]no, [m.] a godfather, a judge or stickler in any countrouersie.' Perceval, *Dictionarie in Spanish and English.*

A Conclusion Touching the Challenger and the Defender

by the same I say prove it, and not follow the other way of Armes. Thereto they are not constrained by necessity and so as they could not by any other means justify themselves.

Those other who are offended for that they have not the lie duly given them, those may wrest the same or by some means lightly reprove it.

OF THE FORM OF CARTELS, OR LETTERS OF DEFIANCE[*]

When cartels are to be made, they must be written with the greatest brevity possible, framing the quarrel with certain proper and simple words. Specifying whether the cause was by word or deed, you must come to the particulars of the same, showing well the persons, thing, times and places which do appertain to the plain declaration thereof, so that one may well resolve to the answer. For the Duello being a form of judgement, as in the civil, criminal and, in action of injury, a particular setting down is required. No less can be said of the judgement belonging to gentlemen and cavaliers, theirs being of no less force. He who shall be Challenger shall call his adversary to the field; he who shall be the Defendant shall join there to his lie.

In such manner of writing the least eloquence and copy of words that may be must be used, but with naked and clear speech must knit up the conclusion.

This I say principally of Defendants, which with superfluous speech most commonly confounds themselves, in that they are not content to have repelled the injury with the lie. They will set down the field and say that they will defend their saying with their

---

[*] A letter of challenge for single combat. See 'Cart['e]l de desaf['i]o'. Perceval, *Dictionarie in Spanish and English*.

weapon. These things are not only superfluous but dangerous, because when one has given the lawful lie, certain and particular, so incontinent is he to whom the lie is given made the Challenger that the proof belongs unto him. He who receives the lie has no choice but to be the Challenger because the proofs belongs unto him, whether it be civil (that is by law) or by Armes. My adversary choosing the proof by Armes, the choice of them comes unto me.

Now if I give the lie and afterward set down the proof of Armes, I enter into his jurisdiction and do the office of Challenger. Whereupon it is most reasonable that mine appertain to his, and seeing that I have elected the proof of Armes, the election of them does not remain to him. For it is not reasonable, nor honest, that I both call him to Armes, and also take the choice of them.

Here I must adjoin another thing. Albeit ordinarily he who has the election of Armes is accounted the guilty, or Defendant, I should say that the same should cease in this case. If peradventure by speaking of Armes I happen to prejudice myself in the election of them, for all that the quarrel does not alter. He who has accused me of any default has to prove his saying, and not I to prove my repulse. Therefore we say that, by the force of the injury done unto me and by me put back, he is to be Challenger. I, for having called him unto Armes, do lose the election of them. Whereupon it follows that he must be forced to prove his intention with those Armes which shall be elected by himself.

Although it seems to me superfluous to remember it, yet it is a thing not to be passed in silence for it is oft to be considered. There must always be held in regard what words they use every time they speak of the fight. The proof and maintaining are taken in the same sense or signification and do appertain to the Challenger. The Defendant ought not to put forth himself but to defend and sustain. If he should offer to maintain or defend, he should become presently upon the same to be Challenger. Of the answers which are to be made unto the cartels there is no more to be said but what is spoken already. In the giving of the lie, the answers yet may be ruled and ordered. When upon the lie there happens no disputation unto him who receives it, there rests nothing but his justification, either unto the proof or satisfaction of the injury.

Here I will not stay to tell you that it seems to me a most gentleman-like thing to speak honourably of his enemy in all manner of writings. For a gentleman, or cavalier, does honour to himself showing to have quarrel with an honourable person. Otherwise he dishonours himself and shows himself rather to have a mind to fight with the pen rather than with the sword.

OF THE MANNER OF SENDING OF CARTELS

Gentlemen were wont to send a glove for a defy and with fierce words did dispatch the same when they came unto the fight. For it was not then among them esteemed peradventure any advantage to be Defendant, not using that (I cannot tell what to term it) witty or cavilling kind in election of Armes, which in these days we are accustomed. Afterwards came the custom of sending of cartels in which manner of proceeding there was much difficulty and newness, and diverse offences to be carried. Lastly the publication is taken up, which is more sure and more ready. Chiefly the lords, having seen the multiplication of quarrels, have provided that in their states no cartels may be presented. This being so effectually brought to pass, every one of them does use it. It leaves no occasion to speak many words upon it. Thus much I say, that as cartels are published and in assurance thereof the day intimated and notified then there is no place left for excuse or alleging of ignorance. By this means all manner of hiding the matter and all other evasions that might have been used in the time of presentation are clean taken away.

This I shall say more, which I have touched on before speaking of the foolish lies. When any man shall give me a lie present and without advantage of weapons or men, if I do not answer him then I cannot hold myself satisfied to come afterward to publish a cartel with the lie. For not being charged, without any supersticery, and I not answering the same and going about afar off to answer him, I do in a manner confess that I am not a man to stand face to face with him. Thus by my deeds I consent that he is superior to me. How shall I, by writing, equal myself to him? My opinion is that such a lie shall never be counted lawful. Truth it is if I do not answer the injurious words presently I am not of opinion that therefore another time I shall be barred to make my answer to the same and to him who gave them me. Only this, I must so hold the same, that thereby I take no advantage in the doing of it.

If one shall be so lame or weak that, answering, it is seen manifestly that the other without any pain may hurt or offend him, to this man it may be lawful to seek assured means to answer. The same in all matters of injury committed with supersticery, although they are spoken to a man's face it is a thing clear, that answering by writing and by the way of publication is an answering to one most legitimately. When the other with another supersticery should answer him that answer shall also be lawful.

A Conclusion Touching the Challenger and the Defender

AFTER THE DEFY IT IS NOT LAWFUL THAT THE ONE GENTLEMAN SHOULD OFFEND THE OTHER, EXCEPT IN THE STECCATA* WHICH IS THE PLACE OF COMBAT

After the one has called the other to the battle, as well in the requirer as the required, it is not lawful that either may offend his adversary any more. For that request or calling binds gentlemen to the ordinary way. Although there should arise among them questions or strife, they must observe this rule: while this question does hang, no other thing is to be innovated. If either of them should assault his adversary in this time, he is to be esteemed, adjudged and declared a breaker of faith, and among other gentlemen from henceforth in any other quarrel be refused and put back. This censure is so universally approved that I need not endeavour myself to confirm it any farther.

WHEN ONE DOES CALL ANOTHER FOR AN OFFENCE DONE UNTO HIM BY A THIRD PERSON

It happens sometimes that one offended with another man's words, or otherwise, makes another strike him or give him the bastinado.† Should he that is struck be called Challenger or the Striker? Unto this demand we have a ready answer. As the civil laws does proceed as well against the one as the other, so in such case the combat being permitted a gentleman ought to proceed as well against the one as the other of them.

---

* See footnote on p.84.

† 'Bastonado: [(Span. *Basto nada*)] a banging or cudgeling.' Blount, *Glossographia*. '*Bastonata*, a bastonadoe, a blow or stroke with a cudgell.' Florio, *A Worlde of Wordes*.

Of Honour & Honourable Quarrels

True, it is said, that when the one has to endure and the other endured, that when the thing is no more but manifest, he who is offended should not leave the certain for the uncertain. Being assured he is oppressed of somebody, his doubt or presumption does not make him apt to require another person of estimation before he discharges himself of him who oppressed him and be offended against him who has with a hand offended him. Overcoming him it is clear that he remains discharged. But to kill or overcome him who required him as principal challenge, I do not see how he is relieved or eased. For the other may always say that he struck me for his own particular interest. The proof of Armes is an uncertain proof, but the stroke is certain. In such case the blame or grief will still remain upon him. Whereupon I resolve to say that the manifest deed of the offence, and not the occult author of the same, is to be called. This assures again that although there are some shows of them a man may also doubt whether they may be false, but there is no doubt of him who is the offender.

⋄⇒◯⇐⋄

WHAT IS TO BE DONE IF QUESTION RISE UPON THE QUARREL, OR UPON THE PERSON OF THE CHALLENGER

Many times it falls out that one calls another unto the field and therefore must accept the defy, but answers the same with some exception. Objecting either that he did not understand the quarrel, or that it does not touch him, or that the caller is infamous, or has other charge, or is not of like condition, or such like. In these cases there is nothing to say except that it is necessary before we pass any farther that such difficulties be made clear. The means to clear them is that the gentlemen submit themselves to the judgement of some prince or nobleman trusted on both parts and chosen by both

A Conclusion Touching the Challenger and the Defender

the parties, and accordingly as they do censure it so the quarrel is to be left or followed.

What if one will not accept the proposed judgement? The opinion of gentlemen shall be of him thus. If he were Challenger, the oppositions made were justly made to him. If he were Defendant, he had an unjust quarrel to defend. When the Challenger should be the man that refuses the judgement, to the Defendant remains naught else to do but to stand upon it firmly. Truly yet, when the Defendant shall avoid the determination, then it appertains to the Challenger to proceed farther. Having shown or sent him the letters patents or of the field, he has more to do. He must send them him and notify them, requiring him that either he accept the one or send back the others, or else let him choose one of them with protestation. If he do not accept the same or refuse to send, he does cause him to understand that he shall avoid it and is to accept such an offer, specifying one of his patents and letters,* and that in convenient time he shall find him in that place or field to make an end of the quarrel with his weapon if he shall be there. Otherwise with all disdain and contumacy† he shall proceed to his infamy, with those clauses which shall be necessary for such an effect.

This is both a gentleman's course and reasonable order of proceeding. If there were not such an order of proceeding found out, everyone would find means to avoid all callings into the fields. Most men would refuse all fighting and judgement, and the required shall remain mocked without any remedy. This remedy is lawful to be used when the Defendant does fly the judgement thereof, that the same should be chosen of both the parties by common accord. When the quarrel is contested and clear, no matter now stands to

---

* A charter from a prince, a writ. See 'Confirmation', in Randal Cotgrave, *A Dictionarie of the French and English Tongues*, London, Adam Islip, 1611.

† 'Contumacy: disobedient.' Blout, *Glossographia*. Stubborn resistance to the reiterated or peremptory orders of a legitimate court, and implied contempt or denial of its authority.

be determined on. If any one article remains to be determined on, they cannot bind another to accept it, nor send patents or letters of the field, for that has his time and place when all controversy is passed. That done, there rests nothing but to come to blows.

Whether the Subject Ought to Obey his Sovereign, being by him Forbidden to Combat

This doubt is often moved by those who write of this matter, concerning which gentlemen are resolved that for their prince and sovereign they will gladly hazard their lives even into greatest dangers, but their honour they will not in any case suffer to be spotted with disgrace or cowardice. Whereby they have grown into this custom – that being challenged to the combat or understanding or perceiving that another means to challenge them, or else intending and resolved with themselves to challenge others, they will retire into some secret place where it shall not consist only in their prince's power to forbid, or stay them from it. They take the combat in hand laying aside all respect of their prince's favour or loss of goods or banishment from their country. Whoever should do otherwise among men professing Armes should be judged to have greatly impaired his credit and reputation and dishonoured himself in high degree.

 He should also be esteemed unworthy to converse with gentlemen, and if chance he should challenge any man afterwards he might deservedly be repulsed, and lawfully. This manner and order are confirmed by long custom and universally approved and held for sterling among knights and gentlemen of all sorts. I think it is needless to trouble myself with answering all such frivolous objections as diverse writers on this subject have made. Whereof,

A Conclusion Touching the Challenger and the Defender

some allege the ancient description of war where it was not lawful for any soldier to combat against the commandment or without special leave of the general. They do not consider the difference of the cases, which is great, seeing it is another matter to be in an army, where a man is bound to attend to especial enterprises than to be idle at home. Besides this, there is also much difference between the defiances used in ancient times and ours. This being in no use or custom and scarcely known unto the Romans, how could they make any laws or take any order concerning them?

Furthermore, those gentlemen or soldiers who in ancient time challenged one another to the combat, being of contrary armies and enemy to one another (whom these writers allege against us) were induced to seek the trial of Armes for one of these two causes. Either the decision of the whole war was agreed upon by both parties to be committed to some few of each army, as it fell out when the Horatii and Curatii,* who tried their valour for the whole armies. In this case it is most necessary that the election of combatants should appertain to the superiors and chief governors. Neither can it by any reason be lawful for each one to take any such enterprise in hand who is willing to do it or else for prose of their valour. Also in this case no soldier ought to go to the combat without licence. Neither does any burden or charge remain upon him if he denies the combat. He is to use his valour in that war not according to his

---

* Arising from friction between Rome and Alba Longa during the reign of Tullus Hostilius (c.672–642 BC) the cities declared war. Before going to battle the kings decided against a full-scale war. They agreed that the war would be settled by a battle between a set of male triplets from each city. The Horatii were brothers from Rome, and the Curiatii were brothers chosen from Alba. The battle was fierce and all three Curiatii were wounded, but two of the Horatii were killed. The third Horatii fled from the battle, and all three Curiatii chased him. In the ensuing chase the Curiatii were spread out and then Horatius stopped running, turned and fought. He killed each Curiatii individually and returned to claim the victory for Rome. For a detailed account see Titus Livius, *History of Rome*, Vol. 1; http://etext.virginia.edu/etcbin/toccer-new2?id=Liv1His.sgm&images=images/modeng&data=/texts/english/modeng/parsed&tag=public&part=teiHeader (accessed August 2013), pp. 22–6.

own pleasure, but unto him whom he has sworn his service and obedience, without any respect of particular interest. Yet it may so fall out that a soldier being burdened with some especial quarrel concerning his reputation ought so much regard the same that he ought to abandon the army, his country and natural prince rather than suffer it to pass unanswered. Concerning this point I will say as much as I can presently call to remembrance.

True it is, that if there rises any quarrel between two gentlemen of two adversary armies they should not challenge, or answer a challenge, without the authority of their general. Without his leave it is not lawful for any man to have any intelligence or dealings whatsoever with any in the enemy's camp. If the quarrel were such that either of the parties should be dishonoured, either by delaying the challenge or not answering the same, then he whose honour and reputation are in danger of stain should so enlarge himself as much as in him lies from that subjection he is in and bring himself into the way whether the safeguard of his honour invites him. Insomuch that among gentlemen this opinion is current, that if a man were in some city besieged by the enemy and could not obtain leave of the governor to come forth, he ought to leap over the walls to go and defend his honour. Yet I will not deny but that, if a man's country or natural prince should be interested in the matter, he should respect both the one and the other, especially when a great part of the quarrel should concern either his country or prince. For then the manner of proceeding therein ought to be platted[*] by their counsel and advice. In all other cases, when the matter only concerns a man's own interest, then any gentleman should not be backward in challenging or answer the Challenger, and in no case either upon commandment, or upon any penance whatsoever, refuse the combat.

---

[*] Planned or mapped out.

A judicial duel

The Angel with a scroll over the combatants illustrates the judgement of God.

According to my simple conceit, neither ought any prince look for anything at his subject's hands that may impair their reputation or work their dishonour.

※

HOW GENTLEMEN OUGHT TO ACCEPT OF ANY QUARREL IN A MANNER THAT THEY MAY COMBAT LAWFULLY

Those who maintain any quarrel most commonly undertake the combat with such intent that although the cause of their quarrel be just, yet they combat not justly – that is, not in respect of only justice and equity, but either for hatred, or desire of revenge, or some other particular affection. It comes to pass that many, although they have the right on their sides, still come to be overthrown. For that God, whose eyes are fixed even on the most secret and inner thoughts of our hearts, ever punishes the evil intent of men both in just and unjust causes, reserves his just chastisements against all offenders until such times as his incomprehensible judgement finds to be most fit and serving to his purpose.

Wherefore no man ought to presume to punish another by the confidence and trust which he reposes in his own valour. In judgement and trial of Armes everyone ought to present himself before the sight of God as an instrument which his eternal majesty has to work with in the execution of justice and demonstration of his judgement.

Therefore if any man violates the chastity of my wife, sister, niece or kinswoman, I ought not or may not call him to the trial of the sword to the end that I may be revenged of him. Nor if anyone should prove disloyal to his prince or country should I to challenge him to the combat in respect of the hatred I bear him, or to obtain favour at the prince's hands, or to purchase honour in my country.

A Conclusion Touching the Challenger and the Defender

Nor if any of my kinsmen or friends were slain may I challenge the murderer to the field, in respect of the kindred of friendship I had with him. My intent ought to be such that although I had not been especially offended, and no particular affection or respect should induce me thereunto, except for love of virtue and regard of the universal good and public profit I was to undertake such a combat. For in all particular injuries I should present unto mine eyes not the persons either offending or offended but rather fall into consideration how much that offence displeases almighty God and how much harm may ensue unto human kind thereby. For adultery a man should to combat, not to revenge the wrong done to one particular person, but in regard to how holy and religious a bond matrimony is, being a lawful conjunction instituted and ordained by God to the end that man and woman therein should not as two, but one person live together in such manner that nothing except death only might separate and disjoin them. Wherefore perpending the dignity and worthiness hereof and how by adultery this divine ordinance and institution are violated, matrimonial conjunction infringed and lawful procreation corrupted, every gentleman ought to undertake the combat. This is not so much to revenge himself or his friends, or to chastise or punish the offenders, as to preserve and keep from violence a bond so sacred and inviolable, with sure hope that God, who (as St Paul says) will judge the adulterer, will by means thereof give most severe judgement.

In like manner, if some man has misbehaved himself in any matter concerning his prince or country, each gentleman should think how God has ordained and authorised princes to be above us, to the end that under him they may as his ministers and officers govern us his humble flock, and how nothing is more grateful and acceptable unto God than good government among men (who assembled together, and living under the same laws, bear themselves orderly, governing their lives and manners aright). We are not so much bound in duty towards any, as towards them who are, as it were, lieutenants unto almighty God on earth, for so I call our princes and governors. Towards that assembly and congregation of mankind, under whose laws we are born and bred, I mean our country, and how no greater wickedness can be committed than for a man to rebel against him whom God has ordained lord and governor over him, or wrong him unto whom he has given his faith, or betray that city unto which he is infinitely beholding for his living, bringing up, and many benefits besides. In respect whereof, I say each gentleman, having considered and weighed all this, should as a public plague, and not as a particular enemy, persecute him who commits any of these odious excesses – calling him to the trial of the sword, confidently hoping and trusting with assured faith that God will chastise and punish him who has so grievously offended both him and his people, violating his sacred ordinances and constitutions. For the same reason if some man has committed murder he who will combat with him must not do it only to wreak the death of him who is murdered, in respect that he was his friend or kinsman. He ought to call to mind what a noble and excellent creature man is, who being taken away and brought to naught by murder or slaughter, the fairest and most notable work which almighty God has framed, is marred and spoiled. Insomuch that whoever commits murder does dissolve and break the most perfect piece of work that the creator of heaven and earth has made and defaces the image and likeness of God. For that, God in his sacred law ordained that man-slayers should be carried from his altar and put to death. The party that will combat knowing how greatly his divine majesty is offended with this sin should not undertake the combat because he would kill him but because he might be, as it were, the minister to execute God's divine pleasure and most holy commandment.

By these examples may a gentleman perceive what should be done in all other cases so that it shall be needless for men to seek examples for each offence, troubling both myself and the reader. In

A Conclusion Touching the Challenger and the Defender

the meantime take this by the way – that whatever I have here said of the Challenger is also in the same manner to be understood of the Defendant, insomuch that both the one and the other ought to regard the preservation of their honour and innocency by just means. The one never challenging but with just cause and upright meaning, and the other never accepting any challenge unless he knows himself to be guiltless. In such sort, he may take it with a good conscience to do or perform any action that concerns his honour, to live and die in defence thereof. It is shameful to do any dishonourable act, so it is more shameful and opprobrious to maintain the same and stand in defence of it.

Again, a man finding himself innocent and wrongfully dishonoured should not fear any danger, but venture his life at all times for the righting either of private or public wrongs and in all things, considerations and circumstances, have a special regard unto justice. God gives right unto him who is just and overthrows the unjust. Whoever therefore shall take Armes for justice to repel unjust injuries may be assured to prevail, and with an undismayed courage go about what he undertakes.

OF
INJURY,
OF THE CHARGE,
AND OF THE SHAME

I have sufficiently entreated upon the quality of lies before and showed the nature of them is to return injuries. Peradventure some will marvel why I should again speak thereof in this place, seeing that the injury must needs be before any return, which (though I confess) is out of order to reduce it under this title. Yet in diverse respects I have been moved thereunto, as namely. I find a very ill custom generally followed in quarrels whereby in contempt of right course and law itself gentlemen are rashly carried to take weapons in hand not considering first if it be a lawful quarrel or such as may deserve a combat, nor do they ever desire to be directed by an orderly proceeding. Gentlemen of discretion should first, before they enter into Armes, rightly examine the quality of their quarrel, if it is worthy of the proof by weapons, and by this means make a right introduction to the truth, so that men are not rashly led on to the slaughter. Again the ground of all quarrels between gentlemen is this, that they think themselves injured or charged, whereof my purpose is chiefly to entreat so far forth as I shall think it needful.

Of Injury, of the Charge, and of the Shame

To begin then with injury, it is nothing but a thing done without reason, as (as we use to say) wrongfully. Charge is no other thing but an enforcing of a man to return, or to prove or reprove anything alleged. It is so termed by this name because the lawyers affirm that the charge of proving rests on the Challenger, whereby it appears that the man charged ought to be the Challenger. Touching these two words, it is to be understood that sometimes both injury and charge are done at one time, sometimes charge without injury, and a man may also injury and not charge. Touching the first thus, I am charged by one with an offence I never committed, wherein he does me injury because he does unlawfully seek to defame me and then lays the charge on me in that he forces me to seek to return the injury and make answer to his opprobrious words, unless I would suffer myself to be shamed. Whereupon I give him the lie and so discharge myself and come to charge him, which sets me free and binds him to maintain his words, which is as much as to urge him to challenge. Wherefrom we are to note that I only charge him without injuring, because my answer is but reasonable, and so the charge rests on him, as I said before.

Injury without charge is of two sorts, viz of words and of deeds. Of words thus: if one man should speak anything of another, which is manifestly known to be false, to this he should not be bound to answer because the first without any return would be accounted a false accuser and a liar. In my opinion it is a more honourable reputation for a man to be silent in such a case than by answering seem to make any account of the words. As a noble worthy man said unto a gentleman who had slandered him, he would neither hold him a friend nor an enemy, nor yet answer his words reckoning him unworthy to be well spoken of by an honest man and too base a subject for a man to speak evil of. If in case of such shameful and false words a man should be urged and give the lie, it is more than is requisite as a thing whereof a quarrel ought not to be taken. For quarrels are to testify a truth and where that is once manifest the quarrel is not required.

Injury by deeds without charge is when a man by advantage or similar means offers a wrong, and it is evident that such a fact was villainously done. This injury I account done without charge in such like sort as that was by words, because if he who is injured would demand from the other a reason of his villainy, how could he otherwise maintain it unless by alleging that the other had taken advantage of him or done him some wrong? If this be so, what further proof is needed? Perhaps some man will ask me if, in this case, he should put up with this injury without revenge. To whom I answer that combat was ordained for justifying a truth and not to lay open a way for one man to revenge him of another. The punishment of such things rests in the prince for the maintenance of peace in the realm, which if it should be severely executed there would no doubt be fewer quarrels by many degrees. In truth, the offence is the greater in this realm where we know God and hear his Gospel daily preached, which expressly forbids manslaughter. By how much he who kills makes a massacre of the very true image of the living God. Wherefore we ought only to fear, reverence and obey him, and not follow our own vain appetites which carry us headlong into utter ruin and destruction.

To return to revenge, he who needs to follow it ought to take another course than combat, albeit many no doubt will advise a man to return like for like, which in no case I would not wish should be followed. Many perhaps who are rather led by an ill custom than reason will wonder at this. I have already alleged, because hereafter I will also affirm, that where an injury is shamefully done not only is the injured free of the charge, but the injurer also rests with the shame. In matters of chivalry, where a man commits no shameful, dishonourable or vile fact, he cannot truly be said to have done unlike a gentleman. I think it an impossible thing to avoid receiving injury from another, therefore when anything happens

Of Injury, of the Charge, and of the Shame

which a man who cannot escape it ought to be judged shameful. A shameful thing is where a man commits villainy which was in his power not to have done. For example, I have power in myself to refrain from injuring another, committing wicked facts, breaking my promise, committing treason, which things if I do not observe I bring upon myself the greatest infamy and shame that any man may possibly bring on himself. His then the shame ought to be who has done this beastly act and not his to whom it was done. This may yet be further confirmed by this argument: where a man proceeds not like a gentleman, he shows a cowardly fear in himself not to dare to maintain it in equality against him whom he sought to have wronged.

Touching this opinion ancient men before us have said that the injury is not his to whom it was done, but his who does it. Again, my opinion is that in case of some former quarrel, he who does any dishonest injury may be denied the combat as one who has before committed a defect. He who receives it should (as the case may be) always be received, supposing always that this defect of him who injuries is manifest.

I will not omit in this place to speak of an ill custom used nowadays, which should no less be confuted by reason than it is commonly followed with great affection. This is when a man knows himself to have rightly received the lie. To avoid the proof by and by he seeks to give the bastonado,* or such like fact, and many times turns his back and runs his way so that he who is injured may not presently take revenge. In this sort he thinks to be valiantly discharged. This likewise the common sort do verily judge and do not perceive their error and how grossly they are deceived. First of all, if for honour sake I would do anything I am to do it honourably and like a gentleman, not villainously and like a traitor. Nor must I think that a shameful fact can grace or disgrace me, but must

---

* See footnote on p. 93.

rest assured that the charge done me by another is yet still upon me, and that I bring a greater shame unto it by this dishonourable deed. Next, if I cannot commit a more odious thing in combat than to run away how may I think to have done honourably by running away? Wherefore should he not be accounted of all sorts of gentlemen more honourable from whom I run than I who run, albeit I have done him some great disgrace? For to injure another is no honour and to run away is a shame. Therefore I will never be persuaded that a man who has justly received the lie can discharge himself by any such act, or that he is not bound to prove that whereon he received the lie, but that he ought to be the Challenger. This opinion I do hold upon the reasons before alleged which I think a gentleman ought sooner to follow than a blind opinion of the vulgar sort which has in it neither law nor reason.

 I would wish gentlemen to examine the causes for which a man intends to fight by these rules and first understand the nature of quarrels, if they deserve combat or if they may be answered otherwise than by the sword, and not to be persuaded by entreaty or favour of any to agree to unnecessary quarrels. Besides the offence towards God, it is an injury to a man to draw him to a fight that is not bound, and it is also a wrong to the magistrate before whom such controversies ought to be decided, intruding themselves into their office and function. Nor yet may we allow a quarrel upon every lie, as I have at large showed in my discourse of lies. We may also note here that a lie lawfully given is that which makes the charge, whereby the other is simply bound to the proof and not to the proof of Armes, because (as I have said before) in such a case where other proof may be made than by weapon the lie does not only not bind a man to the combat, but every gentleman is also bound to desist from the trial by Armes and to rely on the trial by reason.

 I must also add hereunto that every lie whereof a man cannot make justification by civil law does not yet by and by deserve combat. For I would not have any think that there is such efficacy in a lie to bind a man to fight, as it seems some hold opinion. This indeed proceeds from a corrupted use of certain people who have come before us who for want of understanding, without law, reason or right course of chivalry in the beginning, did give liberty to infamous persons to require the combat (as men desirous and willing to behold others in fight) as if it were the baiting of a bull or some other wild beast.* The successors' imitation of their predecessors have brought these things to pass as it is held generally that whosoever he be who receives the lie, be it upon whatsoever occasion, is presently bound to discharge himself thereof only by his sword and not by any other means. This disorder being thus far proceeded should no doubt be carefully redressed so that gentlemen may be reduced from their erroneous opinion by the self-same way and means that they first fell into it. To the end that men may be rightly persuaded, I say that the lie is not the thing that induces the fight, but the occasion whereupon it was given. If there were no proof of the defect whereof a man is blamed then he can in no way bind the other to fight. The regard ought to be the quality of the injury and not the lie.

I am sure some will account this opinion newly upstart. To these I answer that their custom and opinion are far newer, and mine is rather to be proved ancient. No law can be found that commands a man to fall presently to the fight for receiving the lie. All those laws whereon the combat has been granted have expressly rejected the occasions, among which no mention is made of the lie. This is the true and ancient custom approved by the laws of the Lombards,† and by the institutions of the emperors.

---

* Bear baiting was a popular entertainment in England at this time. A bear would be chained to a post in the ground, and then a pack of starved dogs would be released on the bear. It was one of Queen Elizabeth's favourite forms of entertainment. Other animals were also used, such as a bull.

† Compiled by King Rothar in 643, the laws consisted of 388 chapters, which were later augmented by his successors. For a detailed account see Katherine

Moreover, if happily in cartels, there is any mention made that he could prove his intent by civil testimony, yet he intends to do it by weapons. This I say is a very great abuse. Gentlemen ought to take an oath of infamy, that is, that they do not require the field maliciously or with a mind to infame[*] another, but only for proof of the truth. This oath has been ordained and put in practice by men long ago. We must also add that those gentlemen ought to be fully satisfied by an oath from them who demand the field, if that which they pronounce be their true quarrel. Many times some men will not stick to determine to themselves one pretence of their fight and yet make known to the world another.

These abuses gentlemen should diligently take heed of because many times such malice has been discovered. Touching all such matters whereon any controversy or dissension may grow, men especially should beware not to be self willed, but rather take counsel and advice both of their friends and experienced men. If there be cause to judge this course necessary in any matter it should chiefly be in such cases wherein a man's life and honour are touched.

We see that even the wisest people study and endeavour by all means possible to furnish themselves with men experienced and seen in chivalry and Armes who they may be counselled and advised by and may wish them to the field, as may best stand with reason because this office may only be executed by learned men and gentlemen. The first are termed counsellors and the second Padrini.[†] If happily one man be seen in both he may very well suffice to execute both offices, but because the charge consists principally on the Padrini we will speak of them somewhat.

First then my opinion is that the Padrini were so called either because such gentlemen as had remitted themselves unto them ought to account of them as their fathers, or else this mutation of

---
[*] Discredit, impugn, dishonour or slander. 'Infame: infamous, reprochfull, detected, shamed, defamed, slandred, ill spoken of.' Florio, *A Worlde of Wordes*.

[†] Plural of Padrino. See footnote on p. 88.

letters is derived from the Latin which terms those patrones, which take upon them the defence of another. Some also do not call them Padrini, but Pattini. This, if we will allow, must be for they make the math of the combat. However they be called or wherever their denomination be derived, they are very necessary and their very office is to defend as advocates* do their clients. As this is their duty so I think they deserve no less privilege than advocates do.

As in civil controversies, advocates are not to satisfy or play any part of that wherein their clients are bound or condemned, so in reason the other ought not to be charged to the field in those quarrels. They are, but as it were, proctors,† for the injuries, lies, cartels, and challenges that have already passed between the principals. The Padrini speak but as procurators, which is as much as if the principals themselves spoke. If happily the principals should have any words together after the quarrel concluded, yet new charge or lies should be of no force. If between the principals it is granted, much more ought to be to them that speak for them. As it is reasonable so is it to be observed for the better conservation of the right use of chivalry and to the end every man may freely execute his function.

This thing I note, because it happens sometimes that such men take upon them to be Padrini who do it more to take hold of a new quarrel than for the defence of their gentility. This is a wonderful abuse as it has been showed before. The nature of Duello is rather to restrain a man than to give him liberty, being very unmeet then upon one combat should another still ensue. In this respect gentlemen should strictly observe this rule before. As often as any quarrel happens to grow between Padrini, gentlemen ought to

---

* 'Advocate: [(advocatus)] a man of Law that pleads, assists, or sollicits another mans matter, so called [ab advocando], [i.] calling unto, because he is called to his clyents assistance, most properly a Procurator or Proctor in the Civil Law.' Blount, *Glossographia*.

† Attorney or practitioner of law, a counsellor.

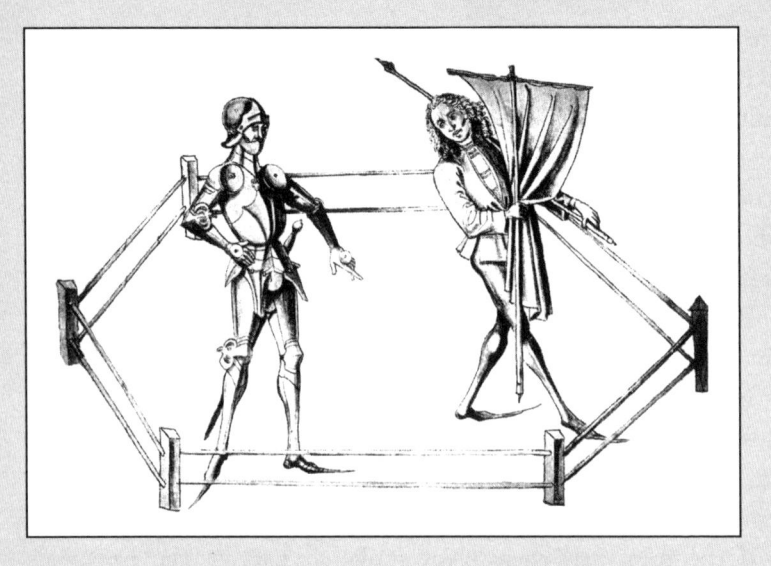

Above: *A knight entering the list for judicial combat. His attendant carries his banner and spear.*

Below: *The knights and their attendants waiting for the combat to begin. Note the coffin next to each fighter.*

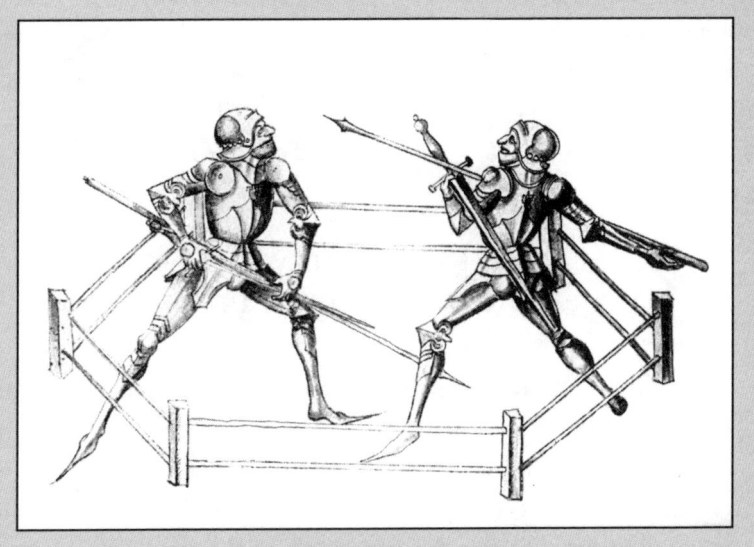

Above: *This trial by combat begins with combatant on the right preparing to throw his spear.*

Below: *The combatant on the left throws his spear which is parried by the combatant on the right.*

condemn it as unlawful and seek to prevent such dishonest actions by all means possible.

THAT MEN SHOULD NOT FIGHT WITHOUT WEAPONS OF DEFENCE

The opinion of our ancients is that whenever any man is licensed to the combat in all other cases, except for infidelity, he is to fight with a staff and a buckler. Whereby I conclude that Duello was not instituted for the honour of chivalry, as our late combaters have wrested it, but only for the sifting out of the truth. This was not done with the weapons of a gentleman, but with a staff. Therefore to go about to reduce our customs nowadays to those of former ages would be more ridiculous than possible to be done. I will only treat of the weapons belonging to gentlemen which I think meet for combats.

First therefore it is to be understood that the wisdom and discretion of a man is as great a virtue as his magnanimity and courage. These virtues are so much the greater by how much they are accompanied with wisdom. For without them a man is not to be accounted valiant but rather furious. Neither is he valiant who rashly and without advice hazards himself in great matters or endangers himself most. He that advisedly behaves himself in the actions belonging to a gentleman and where there is a public benefit or his own honour requires it will not retire himself from danger. For (as a philosopher well says) neither is he valiant that is afraid of every bug, nor yet he that does not temper his fears.

Again, as the courage of the mind emboldens a man to assault his enemy, so wisdom teaches him likewise how to defend himself. I will never hold him courageous if he will be led to fight without

Giacomo di Grassi's frontispiece showing the weapons of a man of arms.

A combatant waiting for a decision.

sufficient weapons of defence. The common sort think these the single rapier in the shirt or the poniard or such like weapons wherein there is a manifest judgement of death to one most honourable. I am not of that opinion, nor will I account them who enter the combat in such sort more honourable than wild beasts that wilfully run upon their own death.

And touching such who think it an honourable thing not only not to esteem their life but to run on their death voluntarily, I will account their life at a very low and base price seeing they themselves set no greater reckoning on it.

It is held a most shameful matter if, when the custody of a castle shall be committed to a man, he shall forsake it without licence. Shall we that have our lives lent us in keeping from our creator have no respect of so goodly a receptacle of our souls but wilfully destroy it, making ourselves as it were rebels unto God and so bring both body and soul to perdition?

Moreover, if a gentleman goes to the wars we see him so esteemed of when he is in show of his armour. Therefore I see no cause at all that in public matters a man should seek to be well armed and in private quarrels come naked. I think a man should at all times and in all places show himself valiant and desire the victory. If it be granted, they should likewise in all matters of moment prepare themselves armed.

If gentlemen will have this respect of courtesy towards their enemy, as to give him weapons wherewith he may end the controversy, I think it reasonable the weapons should be such that may arm him and not burden him.

The duty of every gentleman is to temper his courage with wisdom so it may be known that he neither sets his life so highly that he will commit any vile fact to safeguard it, nor that he regards it so slightly that without just cause he will deprive himself thereof. Albeit I do not account it a dishonourable act to come armed like a man at Armes if the weapons be such belonging to a gentleman and do not hurt a man secretly.

Again I would that Armes should not incontinently be used. A man should not then enter the combat when it is time for him to leave. Above all, the weapons of defence are both weapons of Armes and war. If a man would fight with weapons only of defence the gentlemen should in no case admit it, but that they should fight like gentlemen as it has been done many times.

Touching on the choice of your weapons, the inequality of them and the imperfections of the body. The Defendant has great advantage, and it is not without just cause. For seeing he is both accused and constrained to fight this is a great reason that he should have all the honest favour that might be. It is no little honour to him that in case he only is not overcome he is accounted the vanquisher when contrarily; the Challenger is to overcome unless he will altogether lose the quarrel. Whereof there is great reason. To the one it appertains to prove and to the other it is sufficient only to defend.

Likewise it is as great a favour that the Defendant has to choose the weapons, which is also very meet. For if a man chooses to call me to fight the election of the weapons is mine.

In this choice it is certain that there is not the liberty given for this part as is thought. As all other parts of Duello are grounded upon reason, we will be nice to see how a man is authorised to make the choice.ABC. Wise men are of the opinion that gentlemen should receive their sentence of weapons from divine judgement, if in case the justification cannot by other means be made. If they will have the benefit of that it is necessary that they abandon all violence and deceit, which (as Cicero says) are the properties of the Lion and the Fox and far from the nature of man.*

---

* 'With this I will close my discussion of the duties connected with war. But let us remember that we must have regard for justice even towards the humblest. Now the humblest station and the poorest fortune are those of slaves; and they

Above: *Giacomo di Grassi illustrating 'Della Due Spade' (the two swords) commonly referred to as a 'case of rapiers'.*

Below: *Camillo Agrippa illustrating a sword and shield technique.*

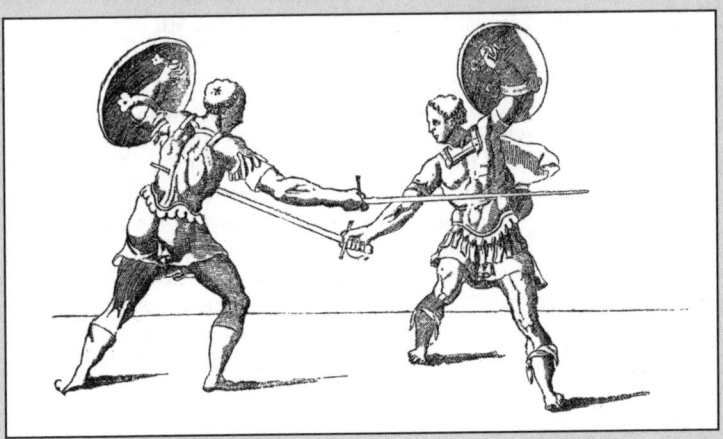

Now if these things should be held and performed in the whole course of our life, much more should they be desired in the sifting out of a truth and in the direction of judgement.

And touching violence I think the law has well provided by giving the advantage of the weapons to the Defendant. If it were not so every naughty man would embolden himself to make wrong accusations and urge every man of less strength to fight, persuading himself to be able to beat him down to the ground. But seeing the law has so well provided against this, seeing that deceit (as the same Cicero likewise affirms) is worthy of much hatred, it is a commendable thing that it is so. For in the choice of weapons it belongs to us to make some law for the Defendant. This should be such that he should not use any deceit in, nor grant such weapons which do not fit with the disposition of a man's body. For albeit a man may say that we are naturally apt in all exercises to use both hands, yet it is manifest that use does overcome nature to make us right or left handed. Therefore if I am known to be right handed I cannot force my adversary to fight with a weapon for the left hand seeing the disposition of my body is not such. If I have no defect in my arm, thigh, or leg I cannot come to fight with vambraces or such like harness,* for those parts which hinder the bending of the elbow or knee. This is an apparent deceit and ought to be refused in the combat. The Padrini should not admit such weapons.

---

give us no bad rule who bid us treat our slaves as we should our employees: they must be required to work; they must be given their dues. While wrong may be done, then, in either of two ways, that is, by force or by fraud, both are bestial: fraud seems to belong to the cunning fox, force to the lion; both are wholly unworthy of man, but fraud is the more contemptible. But of all forms of injustice, none is more flagrant than that of the hypocrite who, at the very moment when he is most false, makes it his business to appear virtuous. This must conclude our discussion of justice.' Walter Miller (trans.), *De Officiis XIII, Marcus Tullius Cicero*, Loeb edn, Cambridge, MA, Harvard University Press, 1913, p. 45.

* Armour.

Of Injury, of the Charge, and of the Shame

If in the case where I am lame or hurt in one of my arms, hands, or want an eye, I may very well appoint my enemy such weapons as may bind his leg, arm, hand, or that may hide one of his eyes in like sort. Yet if he be lame of one arm I may sure appoint him such armour as may hinder the other that is found.

And to conclude, if it be lawful for me to appoint such weapon or armour to mine enemy as may hinder him in the same sort that I am hindered, yet I must not hinder him unless I am also hindered. As thus, if I be blind of my right eye and he of his left, I must not therefore also hinder his right eye. For this is not to make equality of my wants but to take his whole sight from him.

Likewise a right handed or left handed man, or a man so weakened or maimed of his hand as he cannot close it well, or that wants a finger whereby he is not able to hold his weapon in his hand, in my opinion, he is not to be constrained to fight with his imperfect hand but may lawfully and justly deny the challenge. This is also to be understood of all other members and limbs. It is requisite that all things be guided with reason and judgement for both parties so that it does not appear that which is done is done for revenge or to infame[*] another, but only for the justifying of the truth.

OF THE TIME FOR DUELLO

The time appointed for Duello has always been between the rising and setting of the Sun. Whoever does not prove his intent in that time can never after be admitted the combat upon that quarrel. And in case the day is spent without any combat, it cannot be remitted

---

[*] See footnote on p. 112.

to the day following without the consent of the Defendant. He being challenged for that day and appearing there has performed all parts of his honour and duty (unless though any default of his the combat was not attempted) and is far from all matters touching that quarrel. But it is not sufficient for the Defendant only to consent. Likewise the lord who grants the field must condescend thereunto. Having once admitted the field on a prefixed day, that being passed he is discharged. Again, it may be the case that the first day being gone the combat may be lawful done on the second day, but without new conditions. In ordinary course we are to observe that which we said before.

OF ACCIDENTS THAT HAPPEN IN THE COMBAT

As I have already begun to treat of Duello, so I do mean to prosecute it according to our use nowadays. First then, after the combatants have entered the lists, if they have no further agreement between them, whichever one happens to touch the rails or bounds or has any part of him out of the lists is not to be accounted prisoner or have that member cut off. If the fight is to continue to the death, flight, or till it be forbidden then if any of them go out of the lists he is to become prisoner. If his horse is wounded or slain, or if any part of his armour breaks, he is not to be supplied. If he let his weapon fall out of his hand it is lawful for the other to wound him unarmed. I say lawful in this respect, that it is accounted an honour to the other to bid him take up his weapon and stay from hurting him till he has recovered it again. Although in cases where he might have safely overcome the other and victory should afterward happen for the other, he should be accounted a fool and very well served.

Henry de St Didier illustrating 'A prinse faut faire contre prinse comme est icy monstre par ce Lieutenant au Prevost'. It is demonstrated here by the lieutenant against the provost a seizure and counter-seizure (translation courtesy of Maestro Jeannette Acosta-Martinez).

I account these things to be ordinarily observed unless it was otherwise agreed upon which conditions are to be held inviolable under the pain appointed. Even if no punishment was allotted, whoever should do contrary to the agreement is to be held a traitor. This agreement is likewise to be with the consent of both parties. One man cannot bind another to accept any conditions that are outside the limits of the law. I think it is necessary to set down that the Challenger is to give the first assault. Whereas he is to prove and the other just to defend, it is plain that if he does not begin then the other is not bound to stir a foot. Yea, whatever he attempts before he should perceive the Challenger coming to assault would be mere superfluous. Again, at the entrance of the combatants within the lists let it be proclaimed that no man, under pain of death, speaks a word, nor makes any sign. If it happens to be done, he ought to be executed severely and without favour as one who intermeddles in a matter of life and honour of other men.

If Gentlemen being in the Lists may repent them of the combat

Another question is whether gentlemen brought into the field may repent of the combat. I persuade myself that this will never happen between honourable persons. How can a Challenger repent him of ending his quarrel without perpetual shame and dishonour and never be allowed to require battle of any other? He did not prove that to be true for which he once undertook weapons. I would wish everyone who thought his quarrel unjust not to take it upon him. Rather than fight against a truth, make full satisfaction to the injured. This should be done in a zeal and love of virtue. For standing obstinate in his purpose until the time he come to have his weapons in hand and then recant, I think it argues a most vile and wicked mind. I do not see how this repentance can come from the Defendant unless he is content to give over the quarrel and acknowledge himself such as he was accused for. Which (as I said of the Challenger) he might do with less shame before he took up weapons than after. And whenever they should come to an agreement without farther satisfaction, doubtless the Challenger should receive the shame. I do not see how such a case should happen except, in my opinion, if it should be that the quarrel was of a matter belonging to the prince, in another man's interest their honour ought to constrain them to fight, or to make manifest the truth of the fact. If it was touching their particular causes it might be licensed without combat, but not without shame.

WHETHER GENTLEMEN MAY IN THE LISTS CHANGE THEIR QUARREL

I cannot pass over another doubt which is this: Two men fighting together and the one says: 'defend yourself traitor'. The other answers: 'I grant you the first quarrel, and I do now fight with you upon the second'. In this case I think it clear that he to whom the quarrel is refused is the victor. Yet if the other overcome in the second he is likewise to be accounted victor. But notwithstanding, my opinion is that neither of them can depart the lists with honour. They are both blameworthy as dishonourable gentlemen taking upon them to fight in unjust quarrels which must needs be presumed by both their losses. The victory of one cannot take away the loss of the other. Wherefore in this case he who would take up a new quarrel should not say 'I remit you the first', but only 'you lie in saying I am a traitor and upon this hereafter I will defend myself'.

Then if he chance to overcome in this it cannot be said that he has lost the other, but the presumption should be favourable on his side. If his adversary has had the worst in one it is to be presumed the same in the other. He to whom it belongs better to fight on the first quarrel should not condescend to the second, but answer that he will make an end of the first and afterwards speak of the rest. When the other remits the first he is to take advantage thereof and demand of the lord of the field the patent of his victory and not to fight anymore. Nor should the lord himself suffer him to fight again. This is as much as I thought good to speak of that which appertains to the gentlemen.

Now I will come to the office of the lords of the field who, if after the letters of the field are dispatched the gentlemen change their quarrel either in the field or without, may at their pleasure revoke those letters and forbid them the battle. They are not bound to grant the field except upon that special quarrel which was referred to them and whereupon they granted their letters. Whereby also for this cause it should not be unless the quarrel was expressed in the patents.

Again I say that if the gentlemen change their quarrel in the lists without assent of the lords and one be slain the lords ought to punish this fact in the slayer as manslaughter, having killed a man in his jurisdiction without the privilege of a free field. For the field is not to be accepted free and privileged except only for that special quarrel whereupon it was granted. Some men may say that the lord perceiving them to undertake a new quarrel and not forbidding them, seems by his silence to consent. This I will neither affirm nor deny.

Of Injury, of the Charge, and of the Shame

WHO IS NOT TO BE ADMITTED TO THE PROOF OF ARMES

Forasmuch as the Duello is a proof by Armes which appertain to gentlemen and gentry is an honourable degree, it is not meet to admit proof by Armes to any except honourable people. Therefore, as before, civil judges are not permitted so that infamous persons can accuse any other. In the judgement of gentry an honourable person cannot be accused except by an honourable person. For how shall he be able to accuse another of any defect of honour that, in the like, is faulty himself? The use of weapons has been ordained to an honourable end to punish the wicked. How can they be received to this office when they are themselves worthy of punishment?

Therefore it is to be concluded that they are not to be admitted proof by Armes if they have committed any treason against their prince or country, or have had conference with enemies which may be prejudicial to any of them. Nor they who having been taken of the enemy and having means to return do not return, or being sent as spies do remain with the enemy, or have become spies on both sides, or such as having taken oath or have not served out their full pay do run to the enemy, or not having taken oath do go to the enemy at such time as both parties are in Armes. For this fact is the nature of treason because you, making semblance to be in my favour and I trusting you, when it is time that I stand in most need of you, you become a rebel against me.

Moreover, such are to be denied the field as in battle have abandoned their leaders, ensigns or either by night or day shall have forsaken the guard of the enemy or prince who was committed unto him.

To these we may also add freebooters* and all such as for any military disorder are banished. Likewise, all thieves, robbers,

---

* Outlaw, fugitive or rebel.

ruffians, tavern hunters, excommunicate persons, heretics, usurers,[*] and all other persons not living as a gentleman or a soldier. In conclusion, all such as are defamed for any defect and are not allowed as witnesses in civil law are comprehended in this number.

And of these I say that not only are they to be refused upon challenging another man, but all honourable persons or gentlemen should abandon their company. Whoever should fight with them should injury himself, making himself equal with dishonourable persons.

It is very meet that he who will refuse another upon his infamy should be sure that the other is faulty thereof, or that it is so apparent that he cannot deny it. Otherwise he should turn the quarrel upon his own back and then he shall be forced to prove it.

Since it is not lawful for the above mentioned men to challenge another, if they be once challenged advantage cannot be taken against them of infamy. Nor is it meet to accept a man's excuse that should say he did not know it before. For whoever will challenge another should advisedly consider that he binds himself to such a matter as he must not repent himself of.

I do not include in this that if he should commit any infamous act after the challenge, whether he were Challenger or Defendant, he should not yet be refused. Moreover, if an honourable person should challenge a defamed person or contrarily he being challenged by a base person should accept the challenge, this is not only an act of private interest but a prejudice to the degree of gentry. In this case it is the office of the lord of the field not to suffer this combat to proceed nor to grant them letters of combat.

---

[*] See footnote on p. 74

Of Injury, of the Charge, and of the Shame

TOUCHING THOSE THAT DO NOT ANSWER, OR DO NOT APPEAR IN THE FIELD

When a man is challenged to the field he is to answer by weapons and not by words, unless the Challenger is such as with reason he is to be refused. This is provided always that a man cannot defend himself by civil law and that the quarrel deserves combat. But where whoever being challenged does not answer, or without cause does not accept the letters of the field, or accepting them and not having a sufficient excuse does not appear, is to be reputed dishonourable in every man of worth's judgement. The Challenger, at a convenient time, is to appear in the field to use the accustomed solemnities. The day before the combat the Padrino is to come before the lord of the field and tell him that his Champion will come to prove his quarrel. For that cause he as his procurator does appear to see if the contrary party has come and if he intends to capitulate or bring to pass that they may be in the greater readiness against the next day, protesting that his Champion is in readiness and is to beseech the lord of the field to cause inquiry to be made, if either he or somebody for him be present. If there be no notice of his coming he will make open proclamation that whoever is there for the contrary part should appear. If he does not appear it shall proceed against him as one contumacious,[*] and who has failed his duty. This the lord of the field is not to deny the other. On the day appointed he is to appear in the lists at a convenient hour where his Padrino offering him to the lord and showing that his Champion is come to fight is to make a new instance for a new proclamation touching the quarrel. This he is likewise to do at noon and at the evening and withal shall make show of his armour and of his horse wherewith he came furnished to fight. Whereby he shall have cause to accuse his adversary of contumacy and demand that

---

[*] See footnote p. 95.

his Champion be admitted to run to the field and be pronounced victor and the other be condemned of contumacy, of failing, and vanquished in the quarrel.

He who is pronounced vanquisher may use such terms against the other as by the order of gentry is permitted. All these things the lord ought to grant him. The gentleman shall go about the field three times with an honourable pomp of his horse and armour and sound of trumpet and shall carry with him the letters. This being done he may likewise carry the portraiture of his adversary.

And whatsoever has been said of the Challenger may the Defendant in like case do.

WHAT IS TO BE DONE UPON THE ALLEGING OF ANY IMPEDIMENT FOR NOT APPEARING IN THE FIELD

We are now to consider what course is to be taken if any gentleman does not appear in the field at the appointed time nor does not prove a lawful impediment that hindered him. In this case I affirm that first if the impediment happen at such time as notice might be given before the contrary party should appear to the field it is then to be admitted, upon defraying the other's charge and pains and upon the justification to him of his lawful excuse, offering himself also at convenient time to procure a new field and to satisfy any loss which the contrary party should suffer by means of prolonging of time.

But if this should fall out so suddenly as in no sort there could be any knowledge given of it before the very day appointed, yet is the excuse to be approved so the impediment is lawful. He is then likewise to defray the charges of him who appeared. If I make agreement with you to meet you on such a day, at such a place, and

Of Injury, of the Charge, and of the Shame

for such a cause, and I be there present and you be hindered whereby I am put to a new charge, there is no reason that your commodity should return a discommodity and a loss to me. Excuses of lawful impediment should be great infirmities, tempests, or waters that may stop passage, the war of a man's country, prince, or against infidels, and such like accidents which any indifferent judge may think lawful. Imprisonment is also a lawful excuse unless it is such as a man at all times may be freed of. For gentlemen that are to go into the field ought by all means to avoid every occasion that may hinder them from their intent. For whoever in matters of honour does not seek all that he can to salve his honour or has any other respect at all than to his honour, makes a great breach of his honour. Therefore whoever should procure himself to be commanded to stay by his prince is to be adjudged as one that procures his own imprisonment.

I do not allow it as a lawful means to prolong time if after a quarrel is once started a man should take any new charge of office. I would think this sought after to that end and is not to be approved good because being bound in honour he is to first satisfy that before he go about new matters.

Yet I grant that if in this meantime (be it be succession or good fortune) any lordship or great title should befall a man, by means whereof his adversary who was his equal before now becomes his inferior by far, in such case this accident is to be taken for a new and just impediment, not so much to win time as to fight in his own person. For in this case the quarrel begun should be performed by a substitute or Champion as we term him.

IN HOW MANY CASES A MAN MAY OVERCOME IN THE LISTS

The success of fighting in the Lists may happen diversely. Sometimes it may be that the combat enduring to the Sunset the Challenger may neither overcome the Defendant nor be overcome by him. In this case the Defendant is to be adjudged the vanquisher and be absolved of the blame objected him by his adversary. The Challenger shall be accounted the vanquished and an ill Combatant and may be refused if afterward he challenges any man upon any other quarrel. Yet he shall not be the Defendant's prisoner unless the Challenger shall overcome him and only in this one case the Defendant fighting and not overcome does overcome the other. Other cases are common both to the Challenger and Defendant. One is in killing his adversary; another is when a man yields in whatever kind of words. A third is when a man does expressly disclaim from the quarrel confessing himself either truly accused or to have falsely accused. Last of all is the running out of the lists. Of this sort of losing the field everyone is so much the more shameful by how much the more I have placed and set him down in his lowest place or room. To be slain in the field is less shameful, though it is far more dangerous and hurtful.

It may also happen that a man may overcome his adversary or enemy by strength and bind him or hold him in his own power so that everyone watching may judge that he may kill him if he willed it and thereby end the field. Holding him in such sort requiring him to yield and the other not agreeing, it is certain he may lawfully kill him. If he should not kill him and thereby the day be spent, it may be doubted what judgement should be given in this case. If the Defendant be the better there is no question to be made, he is to be pronounced vanquisher although there could not be so full a judgement given of his overcoming as we have spoken of before. If the Challenger should be he that should have the Defendant in his

Of Injury, of the Charge, and of the Shame

power, the matter could not be so easily determined. In this case their articles are chiefly to be considered which may be drawn in such a manner as without any ado at all the matter may be resolved. If it is expressed and set down in them that the Challenger is not to be held vanquisher unless he either kills or make the Defendant deny his accusation, in this case he cannot be accounted vanquisher.

If it be concluded that the Defendant is not accounted vanquished unless he is slain or deny his words I would not then condemn him as vanquished. I would say yet that the Challenger had well discharged his part being in his power to have killed his enemy and if the Defendant would renew this quarrel on any other day I do not think it in any way lawful that it should be granted him. If there should not be any words in their articles touching this point, the one holding the other in his power (as I have said before) I think is less to be adjudged and taken to be his prisoner than if he had yielded himself unto him and so voluntarily become his prisoner, that he should be sentenced to be vanquished and overcome and the vanquisher devoutly and reverently to be esteemed and honoured as one that only satisfying and contenting himself with the victory did not seek or desire cruelly to imbrue his hands in his enemy's blood.

TOUCHING ACCIDENTS THAT HAPPEN TO THE VICTORY OF THE LISTS

He that is overcome in the lists becomes the other's prisoner. He is to have the other's armour, garments, horse and other furniture, whatever he brought into the lists as ornaments for his fighting. This is the right case in this matter for the spoils of the vanquished are the vanquisher's ensigns.

By an honourable custom, the person of the vanquished has been given by the vanquisher either to the lord of the field or to some other prince or nobleman whom he served or followed. This custom, albeit I commend and wish everyone to follow it, yet I must confess that the vanquisher may, if he likes, use his own discretion and hold his prisoner. No man can deny him this because he is to serve him, but not in base offices or in any other way except such as belong to a gentleman. The prisoners taken in the lists may be constrained to discharge the expenses of the combat and they may be ransomed for money even as gentlemen taken in the wars.

THE DIVERSITY OF OLD AND NEW CUSTOMS CONCERNING THE VANQUISHED

I must not omit to tell you that which I have spoken before regarding prisoners has rather been brought in by custom of gentlemen since they began to enter quarrels upon their honour, than by any ancient institution of Duello. By the law of the Lombards he that was overcome in the fight was not given as prisoner nor pronounced infamous thus never performing any quarrel after. He was diversely sentenced for that fault whereof he was accused. As it appears plainly in writing whoever accused for manslaughter was overcome lost one of his hands and whoever was condemned of adultery was adjudged to die.

Touching the witnesses who for consummation of their words did combat, the vanquished lost his hand and his other companions did redeem their lives by money; so severely did they execute the judgement of their Duello. Our learned men allege that because this proof is uncertain albeit a man should in the lists be found in fault worthy to receive punishment, yet he should not suffer death but a mitigation should be used giving him some easier punishment. This as they allege truly and very commendably so is that custom of theirs to be condemned who in case of Duello cause gallows to be set up near the place and do immediately hang up the vanquished. But what greater punishment can there be than that which our laws do inflict upon the vanquished? They do not chasten them in the purse, nor in cutting off any member, not in their life but in that which is dearer than all the rest to every wise man. They deprive him of his honour, for love whereof there is no noble mind that will not spend his blood. Those who go out of the lists vanquished carry away so much more shame by how much they came thither desirous of honour. Not because one man overcame another, for of necessity two fighting together one must be the victor, and (as I have said before) the Challenger not losing does lose so as he is not dishonourable for being overcome but because he is accounted a bad man who would take upon him an unjust quarrel and that he would fight against the truth which he is chiefly bound to maintain. Therefore weighing and considering the great danger those men incur who commit these things to the proof of the sword gentlemen ought to be more slow in fighting, except great occasion urges them and unless they be certain to fight upon justice so they may have great hope to obtain God's favour in it.

TOUCHING THE VANQUISHED, AND OF THE RESTORING OF HONOUR

As I said before so I will say here again, the Challenger who does not overcome his adversary in the lists does remain the loser. He did not prove so much as he ought, so he may never after challenge anyone. This is confirmed with this reason: whoever does not prove

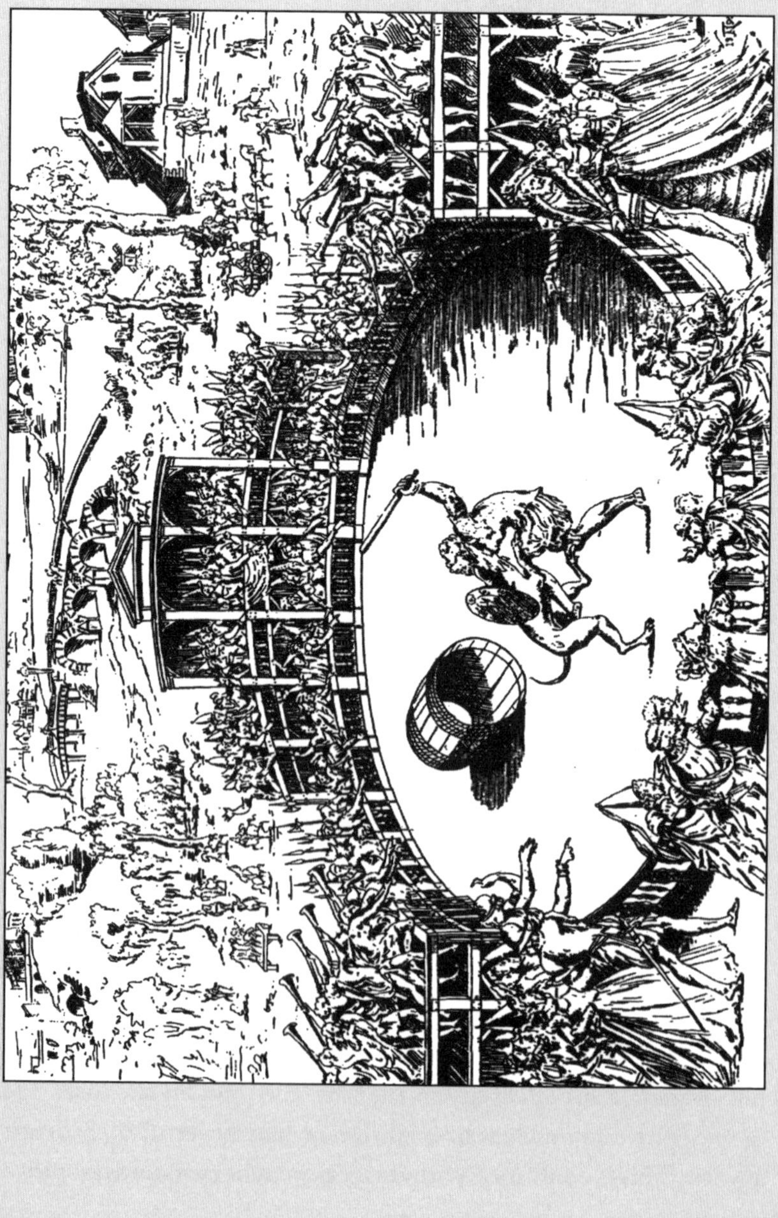

Combat between man and dog

A nineteenth-century engraving depicting one of the strangest 'duels' of all time between a man and a dog. Taking place in 1400 it falls into the category of a 'trial by combat'. The circumstances surrounding a murder led to this curious encounter between man and beast.

The slain victim was Aubruey de Montdidier, who was murdered by his 'friend', Chevalier Maquer, in a forest outside Paris, France. The only witness to this crime was Montdidier's large dog. Maquer buried the body in the presence of the dog. The dog remained at his master's shallow grave until forced by hunger he went to the home of Chevalier Ardilliers, a friend of his master, to beg for food. Ardilliers noticed that there was something wrong with the dog as it whined and whimpered. The dog eventually compelled Ardilliers to follow him into the forest where the animal led his master's friend to discover the grave. Ardilliers and his servants dug up the corpse.

Sometime later, when walking on the street, Ardilliers and the dog met Maquer, and the dog attacked him with such ferocity that it took several men to pull him off. It was unusual behaviour for the dog, as it was known that the beast was of a tranquil and pacific temperament. This occurred again on several separate occasions, which gave rise to suspicion from many people. Finally, all was reported to the king. The monarch made the decision that the guilt or innocence of Maquer was to be decided by a trial by combat in which dog and man were to be the principals.

The combat took place on Île de la Cité, beside Nôtre Dame Cathedral. The dog was led into the lists by Ardilliers, where he was loosed upon Maquer. There is more than one account of what transpired, but this engraving depicts Maquer armed with a stick to defend himself against this large dog. The stick being an insufficient weapon of defence, the dog attacked savagely and seized Maquer by the throat. Maquer reportedly screamed that if the dog were pulled away that he would confess to the crime. Maquer was hanged for the murder that he committed.

his words true is to be thought a false accuser and consequently is regarded and esteemed a bad man. The same of every other man – whether he is Challenger or Defendant – who is overcome by force, made to yield, denies his words or runs away. He can never after that time demand combat nor be allowed it.

I know some who are of opinion that if I overcome one in the lists and afterwards release him, if a new quarrel or controversy befall him with another, by my leave he may challenge his adversary the combat. No man of any reason or understanding ought to consent. If in overcoming him I shall have condemned him as infamous, how can I allow him fit to fight with a man as good as myself? If he challenges me I shall refuse him. I cannot take away his fault that has been overcome by me unless I confess I overcame him wrongfully and so condemn myself of infamy. If I cannot take away his blot from him, then I cannot make him equal with an honourable person. Therefore this opinion is wholly to be reproved of by every gentleman.

As this restoring of a man to his honour is by occasion given me to speak of it brings me in remembrance of the restoring which princes were wont to make of treasons and rebellions done against them and similar faults. Wherein, to speak my opinion, I think it well that although the prince may grant me favour after my treason is committed and pardon of my life and goods and give me honour and a thousand other favours, yet she[*] cannot make that which is done be undone, or the ill fact passed be not an ill fact, or make it that I committed not any treason, or that my soul is not defiled and that I am not any notorious villain. Whatever prince who shall restore me should never trust me, but should rather still presume that since I was once inveigled[†] and drawn to betray my master I will easily be persuaded again to the like. Every honourable

---

[*] 'She', 'her', etc. are used because Queen Elizabeth is the ruler and 'prince' of England.

[†] Seduced or subverted.

means of their loss, cannot be forced from fault of false accusation because they were afterward falsely accused. Nor can they take away from themselves the presumption to be accounted false accusers if they should accuse any man, seeing as they have once before been condemned in the same. In whatsoever sort a man goes out of the lists a loser he is subject to the judgement before given.

After a man has been overcome in the lists once, every honourable person ought to beware not to enter into proof of weapons with him as with all other infamous persons. The same is also to be observed – even being challenged by another he should overcome the second time.

AFTER THE CHALLENGE, FOR SOME CAUSES THE COMBAT MAY BE REFUSED

If, after an agreement of combat between two, one of them should commit some default which brings him into such infamy as anyone stained therewith could not challenge another to the field, he who committed this fault might be refused by his adversary as one who has grown worse in his condition and who changed his nature from that which he was when their quarrel first began.

It is to be understood that this new occasion which a man may be refused the field for should be infamy. A man has fallen into this by his own fault, as treason, false oaths or other notable matters, and not any injury or charge done to him by some other, which might require revenge by weapons. In such case the first who had a quarrel with him might refuse him for becoming worse in his condition. For the second he should not refuse to come to combat with him with whom he entered into quarrel, although he received charge from any other. There is no reason that a man should remain charged of all hands without any means to discharge himself. Therefore he is to take upon him the second quarrel and performing that with honour he may and ought to follow the first.

This is to be noted – the refusal of a man for becoming worse in condition appertains to the Defendant and not to the Challenger. They who are charged ought to seek to discharge themselves and not suffer another man in any sort to take from them such occasion. To be able to do this better let them follow this rule of reason; that whoever is first in time is also to be preferred in way of reason. Because many times one contrary is to be governed by another I will also affirm that if a quarrel depending between two, or the challenge being seen and the letters of the field succeeding, if the one of them should come to such degree of estate and signory that the other were now no longer his equal then might he refuse to be brought to the proof by weapons in his own person among the other. He is yet to perform that by his Champion for the inequality of condition is no occasion to break of the definition of the quarrel.

person should conceive ill of me and avoid my company. It should rather be said that I am restbred* to my goods and the favour of my prince (if happily she will take me into her favour) than to my former honour, because although my prince restores me to all those degrees that she may, yet she cannot restore me to my first innocency. For example, if I be good she cannot make me bad, for it is not in her power to reform my mind. Princes cannot take from good men their goodness nor from the wicked their wickedness. Their power extends on their goods and person but not on their minds. My prince may make me poor or rich but not good or bad, for only God has power over our affections. I conclude therefore that if one who is restored from some notable and manifest villainy would challenge another to combat and this other refuses him, I would judge him to have behaved himself honourably and with reason he might refuse him. For if (as I have said before) a prince's restoring to honour is not lawful I will less think that a gentleman by licensing one overcome by him in combat can make him lawful to fight with an honourable person.

Returning to the restoring used by princes which I spoke of before, my opinion is that it should be good in the children of traitors and the rest of their descendants. They should not bear the punishment of others' offences – especially seeing as those who are baptised are by God's laws freed from the sins of their fathers.

---

* Restored.

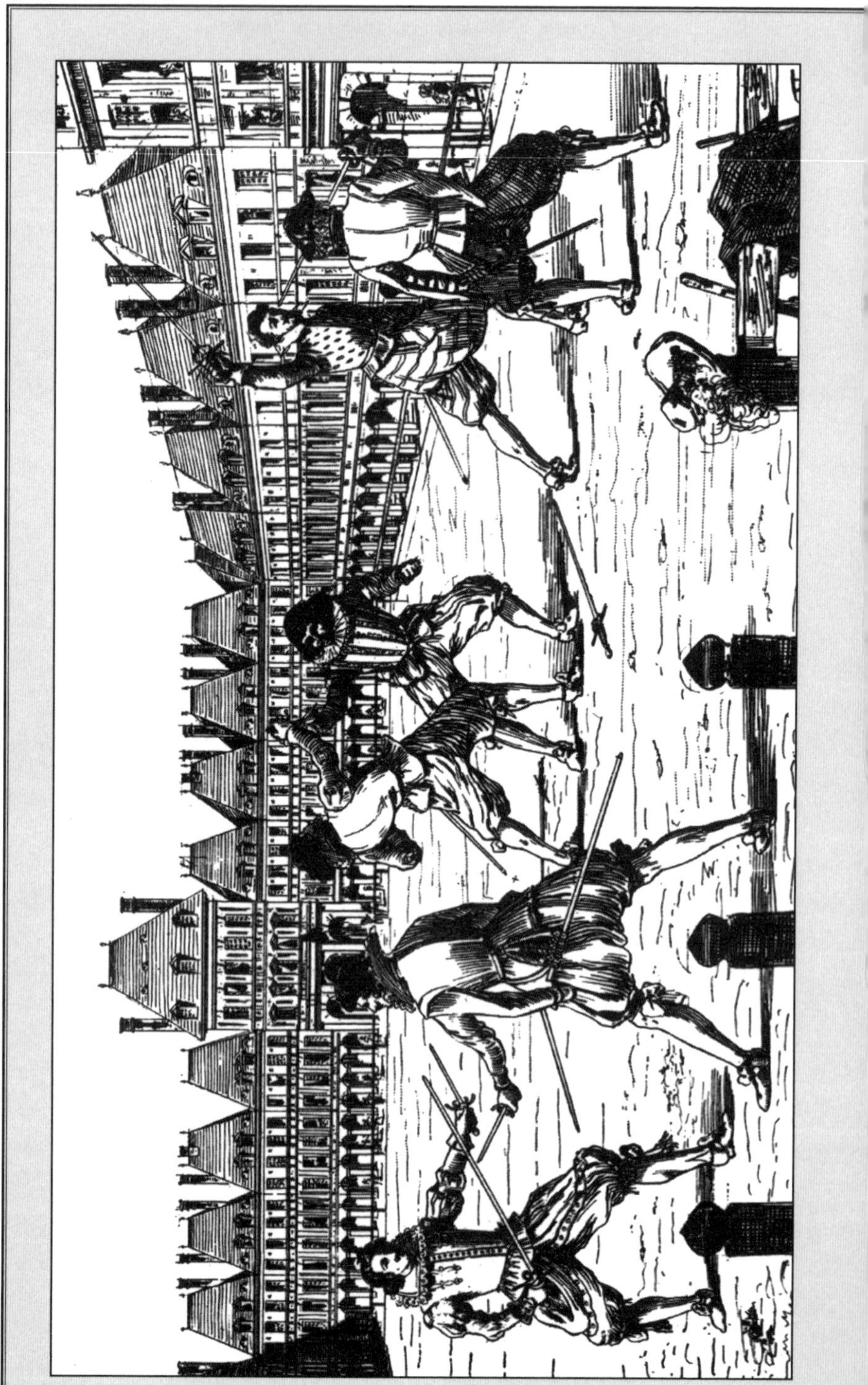

Duel de Bouteville

This nineteenth-century engraving depicts the duel that took place on 12 May 1627 at three o'clock in the afternoon between Comte François de Montmorency-Bouteville and the Marquis de Beuvron on an outdoor square in the Place des Vosges (previously known as Place Royale) in Paris. The Comte de Bouteville was a French nobleman in the court of Louis XIII and was a notorious and unrepentant duellist. Bouteville fought twenty-two duels between the ages of fifteen and twenty eight.

During this era it was the custom in an affair of honour for the seconds to join in the combat along with the two principals. On this occurrence Bouteville was seconded by his relatives, the Comte de Rosmadec and Sieur de la Berthe. Beuvron brought his esquire, whose name was Choquet, and the Marquis de Bussy d'Amboise.

The combat was ferocious and brief. Bouteville and Beuvron fought each other to a standstill and spared each other's life without injury. Bussy died from a wound to the jugular vein. La Berthe was wounded, Choquet escaped to England with the principal Beuvron, while Rosmadec was later arrested along with Bouteville and thrown in the Bastille. Shortly thereafter, both Bouteville and Rosmadec were executed for violating the king's edicts against duelling.

The title of this engraving states that the illustration is based on prints of the time. The two figures on the right are exact copies of an illustration found in the seventeenth-century treatise on fencing, Academie de l'Espée (Leyden, Elzeviers, 1628) by the Flemish master Girard Thibault.

WHETHER ONE ONCE OVERCOME AND AFTERWARD BEING VANQUISHER MAY CHALLENGE ANOTHER

Some men doubting whether one who was once overcome in the lists and is afterwards challenged to fight does overcome is said to have recovered his honour, and after this he may challenge any man to the field. It has been thought that by the honour of his second combating he has taken away the first blot. For the better conclusion we are to think that the first loss cannot be recovered by any new combat. Upon this question I have seen the judgement of Alfonzo d'Avolos Marques of Vasto,[*] which was this. The duty of gentlemen is to prefer their honour before their life, and whoever goes out of the lists the loser shows that he accounted his life more than his honour. Therefore although he should afterwards enter combat and overcome yet it is not to be said that he has recovered his honour. It may be presumed that he came thither with an intent to try his fortune if he could overcome and yet with a mind in all accidents to save his life, because no worse could befall him in honour than had done before when he once lost. Whereas such presumption may be had of him, a man may well think that he came into the field with intent to do anything rather than die. He is in no sort to be said to have revived his honour, which was dead in the dust before. If afterwards he would challenge any man he should be refused.

This was the opinion of that gentleman and this I hold for a gentleman-like opinion, which every wise man ought to allow and follow. This exposition is to be understood, not only of those who confess themselves the losers or run away, but also of those who having had the charge of proving have lost by not satisfying the proof. They, being bespotted with the blame of false accusers by

---

[*] Alfonso de Avalos was the commander of the imperial troops of Charles V in Italy and Hungary and governor of Milan 1538–46.

OF THE INEQUALITY OF NOBLEMEN,

AND

chiefly of commanding lords

This subject of challenging and defending and of refusing and not refusing the field is very large and has need of much consideration. I do not see how a man may truly and fully determine of it without speaking of the degrees of nobility. Wherein I will not call into question what true nobility is because I hold it undoubtedly to be virtue. He is truly noble who is virtuous, be he born either of great or mean parentage, and whoever has not this nobility of virtue, of whatever stock he proceeds, by how much he descends from a more noble kindred by so much will I account him the more base not being able to maintain and keep the honour left to him by his ancestors.

Nobility is seated in the mind and by the mind it is shown. But (as I said before) I intend not to dispute hereof for I have already shown that those defiled with infamy may be refused from proof by weapons. It is always to be understood that nobility is not without virtue, and my discourse is to be in this subject that I speak now of Duello, what degrees of nobility may exercise weapons and by which knights come to be equal or unequal. Athough under the title of knights kings, emperors, gentlemen and soldiers are comprehended, yet there is such an evident inequality between them. Every man knows that a gentleman cannot compare with a king, nor a soldier with an emperor. Although this matter has been handled by many diversely, yet I purpose to speak now about a new and particular manner according to the custom of degrees and worship of our present time.

First then I allege that there are many ways where we may consider the diversity of degrees. For concerning the places of dignity I will first place those princes who are not subject to any other, which I will call sovereign princes. Next to them are feudatory kings,[*] and them I will call most excellent. Thirdly are men right honourable,[†] and after them such as are titled noblemen, under which title I will comprehend all the degrees of worship. These then we are undoubtedly to account superiors to private knights, and therefore as they are superiors to them so are they between themselves unequal. For both noblemen are to give place to the right honourable, and the right honourable to the most excellent, and the most excellent to the free and absolute princes. Besides that, between those of the same title there may also be great inequality. Forasmuch as there is a great difference when one right honourable or noble depends on a free prince or a prince feudatory.

And the same consideration is to be had of feudatory nobility. For one man may assume unto himself the absolute power of a prince, another man can have no greater authority than as an ordinary judge.

---

[*] A king who owes fealty to another monarch.
[†] A gentleman of rank.

Of the Inequality of Noblemen

Besides this we must regard their other qualities and mightiness of signory: for example, if they have vassal noblemen or no, if they hold cities and multitudes of subjects and great port. All these things are to be respected: whether they are free princes or feudatory; whether they are most excellent, right honourable or noblemen; whether they have this honour from free princes or from feudatory princes; if they have noble and honourable men feudatories; and if they possess noble and great state. If we find them not to be much different in some of these distinctions, we are to esteem them equal in the controversy of Armes rather than admit one of them and refuse the other. There can be no greater difference than one is free and the other subject. Only sovereign princes are truly free and all the rest subject in some sort, so we must conclude that as a sovereign cannot be challenged to the field by any man of another degree, likewise those who we have termed most excellent are not to refuse combat with those who are termed right honourable, if they be equal in feudatory nobility and not unequal in other qualities.

The same is also to be held between right honourable and noblemen if their condition, as in the greatness and nobility of state, be not too much different. I see cause to except against any man in controversy of chivalry not to be his equal because only one degree is different between them. As I affirm that only one degree makes no inequality, so I do not allow that one under the title of most excellent may be challenged by one right honourable of the same feudatory nobility, but that concerning his degree he is so far inferior unto him that in another case he would not disdain to receive pension and pay of him. Neither yet will I say that one right honourable should fight with a nobleman although his estate be most noble, nor that one right honourable of great state may be challenged by one noble of small jurisdiction although their feudatory nobility be equal.

I will say that a nobleman feudatory to a sovereign prince, although he is of less degree, may notwithstanding challenge one right honourable who is feudatory to one feudatory and has greater signories. His feudatory nobility does satisfy the other inequalities.

Therefore I conclude in this point that the inequality of persons is to be considered from their titles, from their feudatory nobility and from their states. As they are found accordingly to have greater or less parts equal so they are to be judged equal or unequal.

I will add one other thing, which is this. Although their other qualities are either equal or not much different, yet the quarrel might make great inequality: for example, if a prince, although sovereign, would fight with an emperor for something that belongs to the empire. In such case he might lawfully be denied because the emperor by the condition of the quarrel is true judge thereof and consequently also without comparison of any superior.

OF THE INEQUALITY OF PRIVATE NOBLEMEN

Gentlemen who are nobly born are either without any degree or else bear office or dignity as the government of cities, embassies or commandments in the war. Touching those who have authority, either their office is for term or for life. If for term, then upon any quarrel to be decided by Armes it may stay the execution of their office. If for life, and his degree is such as makes him superior to the other he may fight by his Champion. If his office is not of such quality, he who has the charge of it is to endeavour the good favour of his lord to grant him to satisfy his honour without losing this office. If he cannot obtain it he is to abandon all things and resort thither whether he is challenged or whether his honour urges him to challenge another. For as a man is not bound to anything

Of the Inequality of Noblemen

more strictly than to his honour, so is the lesser to give place to the greater.

Now in that a man is born noble he is equal to all knights of private condition. Although one man was born of a noble house or right honourable, being without jurisdiction or succession of signorie he may be challenged in the field by any private knight.

Moreover, forasmuch as the art of war is a noble exercise and because many mean men have greatly advanced their houses by it, he who shall exercise the art of weapon, if he be without infamy or do exercise it without abuse, is to be reckoned and accounted among noblemen and knights.

I would not that any man should upon this think himself made honourable for having been in the war once and having taken pay and served two or three months without ever drawing sword, seeing enemy or hearing sound of trumpet. This was as much as to dream upon the hill Parnassus that he is a poet and in the morning find himself not so. It is expedient for any man of unnoble who would become noble to get this nobility by Armes, and it is meet for him who would be accounted among knights to do the act of a knight. It is required of a man to make honourable proof of his person more than once, to continue long in the wars, to be known as a good soldier and to live honestly in times of war as well as peace. In such sort it may be perceived he intends only to be a soldier and to make that his principal butt and drift.

If in the study of letters a man does not attain unto any degree of honour or nobility but with pains and watchings of many years, let him then think likewise that hopes to ennoble himself by Armes to sweat often, to endure many heats of summer and cold of winter, to watch many nights, to sleep many times in his armour upon the hard ground, to spend his blood and by many hazards of life to manifest his prowess to the world. When he shall have performed all these things, then he may think himself truly noble (for those are noble who deserve to be known for their deeds) and that he cannot be refused for want of nobility.

Now among soldiers, a soldier may fight with all sorts of men – as the heads of the squadrons, servants and others under the degree of their captain – for his authority represents signorie. They may also challenge them, and they are to answer them being about any enterprise and having degree by a Champion, but being returned to their private condition I see no cause why they should not answer in person. One captain may challenge combat of another unless they be so unequal in place, as one may command the other.

This is to be said of all sorts of soldiers, foot as well as horse, adding moreover that a man of Armes having been in honourable and continual exercise of war, and living in all points as beseems a man of Armes, challenging a particular captain of foot is not to be refused nor he refuse any soldier serving on foot.

I am of opinion that a captain of foot might challenge a captain of horse, but only for the most part those places are bestowed on noble personages, and the conducting of men of Armes is also bestowed on right honourable men. Therefore in this case all conditions are to be considered along with the quality of the enterprises they have. For a captain of foot may have so honourable a degree or be of so honourable family that there could be no cause to refuse him.

This which I have spoken touching captains of foot, or horse, and of men of Armes is also to be understood of footmen between themselves and horsemen also, whether they are men of Armes or light horse. Besides their degrees of greatness in war their degrees of nobility which we have spoken of before in our treatise of noblemen (if they have any) are to be considered and, according to their greater or less inequality, they are equal or unequal. This general rule being given may by men of understanding easily be applied unto particular cases.

Of the Inequality of Noblemen

WITH WHAT PERSONS A KNIGHT OUGHT TO ENTER COMBAT, AND WITH WHAT HE OUGHT NOT

We have long waded through this spacious discourse of chivalry seeking to set down who ought to be denied combat. This matter is so large and copious that if a man was particular to every minute discourse thereof it would contain a greater volume than I intend to make in the whole subject of Duello. It suffices me to have pointed at the fountain where water may be fetched and conclude with my opinion touching the duty of a knight. Earlier I described two important topics: that is who should be clean thrust from combat and who should only be refused.* In those two almost all controversy of persons who enter or do not enter Duello are contained. Forasmuch the wicked and infamous persons ought to be refelled† by knights. They may be refused whose conditions are unequal. If a man would ask why we have not said all are contained in these two headings, well almost all. It is for those which we have spoken before, of learned men and clergymen, who are far from the lists. Not as refelled, not as refused, but as privileged and as such to the quality and estimation of whose condition it is not meet neither to challenge nor be challenged to proof by Armes because their study and exercise are far from the valour of the mind.

To return to our headings propounded before I say that to refel the infamous and wicked is the duty and band of chivalry. For a knight is bound to do so that he does not bring in to the exercise of Armes persons unworthy to appear among honourable persons if they have made themselves unworthy by their own fault. Nor is there any credit to be given them in the proof of Armes which is not received in civil testimony. Neither are dishonourable people to enter into battles that are undertaken for honour's sake.

---

* See p. 128.

† To prove false, refute. http://www.merriam-webster.com/dictionary/refelled/.

Of Honour & Honourable Quarrels

If any knight should make a quarrel with any person incapable of Duello, the lords (as I have said before) in right of chivalry are not to suffer the field to be dishonoured and should not grant the combat.

The refusal is not of band of chivalry but of will of knights, because if a man will not enter combat with one of less condition than himself he may lawfully do it by appointing a mean Champion to decide the quarrel. If a man would not respect degree but would fight in person with one who for his condition or other defect was not his equal, he could not be said to do wrong to chivalry but rather to honour it. Chivalry is not the account of condition but of valour.

In the disputations of arts and more noble sciences no man's lineage is respected but by his worth. Therefore a man of base or high degree may be valorous, and the honour of the lists is not so much for overcoming one born of noble family as one who is known as a valiant man.

Again as great men account it no shame to be called knights with meaner men, so they ought not to be ashamed to come together to do the oath of chivalry. If a man born of a great family has no respect to injure another, I know not why by reason of his nobleness in blood he may refuse to defend the same and to maintain it against him whom he injured. In cases that combat was to follow upon it my judgement is that the injurer or offender, howsoever we term him, is to answer the other in person. Therefore as I think it a discommendable thing for an honourable person to agree to make himself equal to a person who for his vices were odious although he descended of a noble race, so I repute it a knightly course not to be too curious in the difference of conditions especially when they are not so diverse as may seem that the frog strives to be equal with the ox (according to the tale).*

---

* A fable told by Aesop. The moral is that pride and envy can make people believe they are more than is truly possible and this is often the end of them.

Of the Inequality of Noblemen

I will add another case. As I will commend him who should not so much respect the condition as the valour of him with whom he had quarrel, so I would blame him who being of a base estate would compare himself with every great man and would not acknowledge nor content himself with his own condition.

This I speak not only of those who are born meanly but also those born of noble blood who want to be equal with right honourable personages in a private condition and in questions of honour. If they esteem so much of themselves for having blood and being in the families of great lords they are to consider that those lords have ennobled those houses, and they have received their nobility from lords. If they have received it from them, they are by so much less than they by how much he is greater who gives another man nobility than he who receives it.

TOUCHING THE APPOINTING OF CHAMPIONS

We have shown great inequality of noblemen where the lesser cannot bind the greater to answer him in person. No man's greatness can make it lawful for him to unjustly oppress the lesser without leaving him sufficient means to revenge himself. No man ought to make the shadow of his nobility a pretence to be able to secretly commit defects without yielding reasons for them. It is very necessary that as in them there is respect for the degree of nobility so also it should be of honour and justice to provide a meet remedy for every private person. The law of chivalry should be inviolable, kept as well for the great as for the small. Therefore all such as by reason of some excellent degree of nobility shall be found not bound to come in person into the lists with another are also to know that in question of Armes, which they shall happen to have with persons, although private, that they shall be bound to appoint a Champion. Being lawfully overcome or yielding, he who appointed him for his Champion is likewise to be said overcome.

In this point I will deliver the opinion of doctors. In cases where combat is to be done by a Champion, those who present him should also be present themselves and be held under safeguard, to the end that a mockery is not made of Duello and if their Champion loses the field they do not escape the judgement.

The same is also to be done when the quarrel is such that the loser should be condemned in corporal punishment. But where other punishment is not requisite then to be the vanquisher's prisoner may sufficiently suffice, that security be given of the charges and convenient ransom.

The laws of giving a Champion are these: such ought to be given as are not infamous and are equal to them against whom they are to fight. When one party should intend to appoint a Champion, the other may likewise appoint one. It is meet that he who will take benefit hereof should use such course in his writing that he does not lose his prerogative, or jurisdiction as we will term it. If a man by his writing should say that he will defend the quarrel in his own person and afterward appoints a Champion, the contrary party might refuse it with reason.

Again it is to be understood that on either side the Champions are to swear that they think to fight in a just quarrel and that they will do their utmost as if they themselves were interested in the quarrel. Whatever Champion shall willingly suffer himself to be overcome is to have one of his hands cut off, and the adversary has not overcome but the combat may be renewed. After a Champion has been overcome he may not after that fight for any other, but for himself he may.

I will not here omit that although nobility does privilege the greaters to appoint Champions such yet may the cases be: not only a great man with an inferior, but a master with his servant, and a prince with his subject is bound to fight in person. For seeing that promise is a band which equally binds the prince and subject so no greater or less band has the one than to the other. Whenever one man shall oppose unto another any defect of promise and faith he cannot use his Champion. The accuser is to try the quarrel in person with the accused. Therefore when a lord shall accuse his subject or his servant of whatsoever condition he is – violating his faith, women or treason against the state – he is to prove it in his proper person. The same is also to be observed when the subject or servant shall accuse his lord.

Many lords have no care nor consider not the oath and obligation of faith which they have towards their subjects, but reckless of their faith do incessantly commit new defects every day. Perhaps they think that their greatness does cover their defects and do not perceive that by how much they are exalted above other men by so much their faults appear the greater. Whereas both by their example and laws they should instruct others in their life, they opposing themselves against laws give other men example of wicked living. Therefore seeing that the defect of faith is a defect so great in lords it is great reason that they should have no privilege in quarrels of faith. If it be not granted to lords, much less is it to be granted to persons of other quality or condition.

It is to be further understood that besides the inequality of nobility there are also other manner of cases in respect of persons who can lawful appoint Champions. For example, if a man shall not be of eighteen years, or if he be decrepit, sick or in such sort hindered in his body as he is not fit to fight.

OF THE DUELLO OR COMBAT

How and in what manner the Duello or combat has been used they who have turned over the records and annuals of passed ages may know. Seeing it is now long since out of custom and not permitted by the laws I think it is not necessary to speak much in this place. I will only say this, that in times past it was held in very reverent account that gentlemen thought it an honourable quality to be able to discourse on those points and rules that were agreed upon among princes and approved by them concerning free and open combat.

My intention is to give gentlemen warning how they appoint the field with their enemies seeing it is not permitted by the laws to be done publicly as by ancient custom it was wont to be allowed. It may so fall out that a gentleman having passed his word to meet his adversary in some secret place after he has valiantly wounded him and reported the victory of him in the appointed place, his said adversary may accuse him of felony and say that he robbed him, and though the quarrel should have an end he shall be forced to enter into new troubles and begin again. It may also so chance that his adversary has ambushes prepared for him and so he may be murdered. Once dead his enemy may vaunt of having bravely conquered him by right and valour.

I have myself known in countries beyond the seas two captains, the one named Faro, the other Montarno de Garda, the Lord of Mandelot, governor of Leon. They met together where the one, treacherously minded, prayed the other to show if he was privately armed. As soon as Captain Montarno opened his doublet Faro presently ran him through. Seeing him fall down dead (as he thought) on the ground returned into the city with counterfeit glory as if he had done wonders. Until by chance the poor captain was found by his friends yet living to betray the other captain's villainy. Many similar examples have happened and not so far hence, but many undoubtedly are acquainted with them.

Of the Inequality of Noblemen

I would in like manner advise gentlemen of an evil custom which of late years has installed itself among men of all sorts and nations – that is, to be delighted with broils and hurly-burlys and set men together by the ears causing quarrels between friends, neighbours and kinsfolk. Whereas it was wont to be a matter of great consequence and of such nature as it might not be otherwise decided which should bring men so mortally at defiance as nothing but the sword could finish the quarrel. Now upon every occasion Armes are taken, and one friend for a word will not only violate the sacred respect which should be zealously observed in friendship by turning their familiarities into strangeness, their kindness into malice and their loves into hatred, but also accompany this strange and unnatural alteration with a wicked resolution of seeking one another's overthrow, not resting till the enmity be confirmed by fight and that fight ended by death.

Oh the reverent esteem and account wherein former ages had for the combat! And why? In truth because no gentleman sought the ruin or destruction of another and never undertook trial by the sword except in defence of his innocence and to maintain his honour unfeigned and blotless. Now malice and hatred overruns all. Strife and rancour are the bellows of quarrels, and upon every light cause men enter into more actions of defiance than for any just occasion offered in respect of justice and honour.

One more fault, beside these which I have already mentioned, has fairly grown among us. If any of our friends say to us but one word to this effect, 'Come will you go with me, I must fight with such a one and I know not what partakers he has,' we are presently ready not only to go with him ourselves, but to draw others into the mind with us without any consideration of the manner of the quarrel, how justly or unjustly it grew, and so often we bolster wrong against right. We should enter into examination of his cause, learn the quarrel and search for the occasions and causes of their falling out. Being acquainted therewith, though we find him to have reason for his rage (for I know not how else to term that passion that leads men to that mortal resolution, upon whatever just occasion), yet ought we not to accompany, nor to further him. No, do not suffer him to fight if the matter can possibly be taken up and ended by any other means. Such a dangerous trial, in my opinion, is to be reserved for such occasions as necessarily require it. What or how many there are, I leave to be perpended and considered by those who can best discern matters of so great weight, so I will come to those points which I imagine it will not be amiss here to discourse of.

TOUCHING THE SATISFACTION THAT OUGHT TO BE MADE

between Knights

Seeing we have already treated sufficiently of Duello as far as is necessary for a knight to understand, I think it is also very convenient to speak somewhat of the satisfaction which is to be made when a man knows he has wrongfully injured or charged another. Before I proceed I must greatly condemn an old and common opinion which is this: that when a man has done or spoken anything good or bad he should defend and maintain it for good. This opinion, how it is to be approved, I will lay open for every man of understanding to judge.

Forasmuch as man is principally distinguished from brute beasts by his reason, whenever he shall affect anything without reason and with violence he works like a beast. He is transformed even into a very beast as those afore time did very well understand when describing men metamorphosed into beasts signified nothing else but that those men had done acts proper to those beasts whereof they termed them to have the shapes. Now then, if men be turned into beasts by doing like beasts we may also say that as long as they abide in that form they continue in that action or opinion and their abode in that is so. They have no other means to dis-beast themselves (as I will term it) than by acknowledging their fault, by repenting and making amends thereof. A man should strictly follow reason as the chief guide and mistress of his life. If happily he should happen to offend at any time (as it is common to man) he should with all possible speed recall himself, seeing it is a heavenly thing to make amends.

To speak particularly of matters of chivalry, we take the office and duty of this degree to be to help the oppressed, to defend justice and to beat down the proud. Some, quite contrarily, turn their sword, the ensign and Armes of justice, to oppress reason, to commit injustice and to confound the truth. This wicked opinion and perverse custom are so rooted in the common sort as they account it a base thing for a man to proceed with reason and to consent to equity. Although there are many who follow this corrupt use, yet the better sort of spirits do approve that sentence which is preached. I have heard of signor Luigi Gonzaga* who died captain of the Romish Church whose valour has been so well known as no man ought to think that ever he was stayed from any noble enterprise through the baseness of his mind. He was wont to say that if he should be known to have spoken or done any bad thing, the which he was challenged to prove by Armes, rather than fight for the false against the truth and for the bad against the good, he would freely disclaim from it and deny it.

This no doubt is to be held a manly and a Christian-like deed. Reason wills us to do so, and law and the duty of the degree of

---

* An Italian aristocrat born 9 March 1568. In November 1586 he became a member of the Society of Jesus (becoming Aloysius Gonzaga). While still a student at the Roman College, he died taking care of plague victims on 21 June 1591. He was beatified in 1605, and canonised in 1726.

chivalry require it. All doctrines, philosophical as well as Christian, teach us the same.

~~~

WE ARE NOT TO FOLLOW THE OPINION OF THE VULGAR

We see that the earth does naturally bring forth venomous things, thorns, herbs and plants either not profitable or hurtful. All this as a mother she does nourish without any help of man's labour. Those who are good, profitable and helpful she receives with noisomness* like a stepmother, so they have need of continual culture and yearly renovation. That which we see in the seeds of the earth is likewise seen in men of good and bad minds. Through our natural corruption the bad is conceived, received and generally embraced by us all, whereas the good is unwillingly received, and we stop our ears lest we should hear it. There belongs great study to understand the truth, and many pains to bring it to pass so that our minds are capable of it. Therefore by how much the pains are greater, by so much is to be said they are fewer who have true knowledge of the truth. In this respect it is no marvel if the vulgar opinion be so far from the truth.

Learned men have distinguished man's condition in three sorts: the first, such as of themselves are apt to seek out the truth and they are termed the best; the second, such as finding themselves unapt for so good a work do obey others who truly admonish them and they are called good; the third, such as neither themselves know, nor will hearken to others and they are fitly called bad. Seeing that every man cannot be in the first place, yet we ought to believe such men whose authority and doctrine we find approved to follow

---

* The quality of being noisome–noxious to health; hurtful; mischievous; unwholesome; insalubrious; destructive.

their direction and take heed lest through our obstinacy we fall into the last degree, which is the wicked. This we are to perform in all manner of our living so it is expedient to do the like in the order of things of chivalry, abandoning the vulgar opinion and following the steps of those who by valour and knowledge have laid open unto us the right way, and governing us by the laws of reason, and not after the vanities of those who rather by chance or by violence than by any true course or judgement of true understanding do rule their own actions.

OF SATISFACTIONS IN GENERAL

Knights taking upon them to deal of peace chiefly ought to provide that there is hope of the continuance thereof. They are to do this with the least grievance that may be of both parties, not burdening the one for the ease of the other. Many times such things are demanded as are heavier to the offender than ease to the offended. This is not a token of seeking peace but revenge. Yet it is very meet that when one is grieved in anything, the other who has done the wrong should be grieved alike. If you take from me, my reason commands that you make full restoration to me even with part of your own.

Two things are not commonly considered in wrongs committed: the thing whereby a man is wronged; and the manner it was done in. From the deed comes the injury, and from the manner comes the charge. For example, Henry gives the bastonata[*] to Edward when he had no cause to take heed of him, and after he has given it runs away. In this action the stroke is the injury, and the charge is that

---

[*] See footnote on p. 93.

Touching the Satisfaction that Ought to be Made Between Knights

Edward is bound to prove that he did it shamefully. To make them friends Henry will say that he did Edward this injury unaware of him and when he had no cause to beware him. After he struck him he went his way in such sort as Edward could not make sufficient revenge and he is not a man of equal degree to charge him, nor wrong him more than the other is to wrong him. By these words manifesting the manner how he wronged Edward he discharges him from the band of proving this act to be villainous. There needs no proof of that which is apparent, so as all the injury rests on him for which, be he great or mean, it is an ordinary matter to ask him forgiveness.

Moreover the words according to conditions, the age and profession of the parties may alter and change it so that it is referred to the judgement of the meaner. Some men would have it that a man should confess to have done badly or treacherously for saying or doing such a thing and do not perceive that the signification of these words is when a thing is done in a bad or evil manner. Therefore I would not have any man make more account of words than of the meaning of them. After that by the meaning the offended is discharged to seek other words, is not to unburden himself but to burden the other more grievously. Because there are two sorts of injuries – the one by deeds, the other by words – we will severally entreat of them both.

OF SATISFACTION OF INJURY BY DEEDS

I know many are of the opinion that satisfaction cannot be made by words for offences by deeds. I am of a contrary mind, for this is not merely to be considered from words to deeds, but by the grievousness and greatness of the shame that comes to him by the deed and the words, by the shame he accounts to himself and that comes to him from others. For which will we repute more honourable or more shameful: he that is treacherously wronged, or he that commits it? I also mean the same of disadvantage, by striking one behind and other ill manners of outraging others.

In this case I think there is no doubt. Neither is his shame the greater who did the injury nor his who received it (accordingly we have said so before). If I confess to have committed a defect, and through my confession you are justified from not having done amiss, why should you not be satisfied with asking for forgiveness? In my judgement I cannot conceive of any injury so heinous that such a satisfaction may not suffice, especially seeing it has ever been the use of most gentleman-like minds willingly to forgive. Forasmuch as there wants not such who, in case of grievous injury, would that a man should secretly be committed into their hands and discretion. I do not see how it is the ready or honourable way to make agreement. If the offended should take satisfaction by his own hands it seems he deals discourteously.

By such manner of proceeding we have seen that quarrels and enmities have not been ended, but redoubled. If without other demonstration this remission be accepted for amends the matter gives suspect of a secret agreement between them, which is prejudicial to the honour of him who is wronged. If one man should unadvisedly against his will offend another and finding his error he should yield himself and give him his sword and put himself into his hands, using all humility and sorrowfulness then he who was wronged without further adieu should embrace him and lift him up. I would account it a most honourable act between them both. The matter once waxed cold and dealt with by means, I cannot think that agreement may be made by remission. To confirm that which I said, that words may be sufficient satisfaction for injury by deeds, I allege that if happily one man were mightily outraged by another and should write to him that he meant to prove that he had done a vile act and like a bad man and ill knight, if the other answering him should confess as much it is certain that no further quarrel should remain nor band of honour between them.

Yea, and if this come to the lists in making the articles between the Padrini, the Padrino of the challenged should agree to the form of the quarrel and confess that to be true which his adversary alleged. If the quarrel should cease, the combat likewise should cease. If it be so, as indeed it is, I do not see why if those words in the cartels and at the field may satisfy me, the same words should likewise satisfy me in the presence of honourable persons and the same being spoken by mine adversary and he also asking me forgiveness. With these reasons I do firmly conclude that words may satisfy injury by deeds.

OF CONTRADICTING CERTAIN VULGAR OPINIONS OR MATTERS OF SATISFACTION

We have shown before how greatly they are deceived who hold the opinion that after a man has done or spoken anything good or bad he is to defend and maintain it for good. In the section 'Of satisfaction of injury by deeds', above, we spoke of the falsity of that other opinion that satisfaction cannot be made by words to injuries by deeds. Such as do stand in that opinion, alleged authority from general captains, were wont to say: 'Have you struck him? Let him do what he likes'. How far this saying is worthy to be approved may be perceived from that which we have already spoken. I do not think any man of good understanding (if he shall truly know that he has struck another, either with his hand or cudgel) to make peace will say that he wronged him like a traitor or shamefully. We have individually discoursed before on either of these opinions. Now entreating of them both together I affirm that from them may be known the falsity of vulgar opinion so by common consent they are received for good. Yet if we will with sincere judgement consider them we shall find that one of them does repugne the other. If I ought to maintain for good all that which I shall have done, I shall not be able to with my honour say for the satisfaction of him who is wronged – not only all that he will have me say, but not so much as any one thing. If I may say that which he will, it shall not be true that I ought to maintain for well done all that I shall have done. Now seeing that so manifest contrariety is comprehended from so open contradiction they should also perceive their error, and perceiving it reclaim themselves from it. Especially considering that as these two opinions are contrary between themselves, so reason is contrary to them both and that surely is a commendable and gentleman-like opinion which is founded upon law and reason. According to this opinion are honourable people to frame themselves desirous of valour. Not one thing is to be esteemed valorous or honourable if it be not accompanied with reason.

OF SATISFACTION TO BE MADE UPON INJURY OF DEEDS

Speaking in particular of satisfactions that are to be made, the foundation of them is to be upon truth. Whoever has done wrong should confess it. Whoever has reason in it should maintain it. Therefore whoever being moved with just disdain and just occasion shall conveniently revenge himself against any man – he is not to make any other satisfaction than to say that he is sorry to have had occasion to have used such an act against him. If he had done it without cause he should have done ill or like a bad man, or not like a gentleman, or knight, or such like words, and he may also entreat him to be friends with him. He who has given cause to the other thereof, acknowledging his fault should content himself with as much as reason requires and not continue in his error if he will not (as was said before) remain transformed into a brute beast.

If upon any words two should fight, and one of them should be hurt it should not be doubted that they might be made friends without further adieu. Blood does wash away all blots whichever of them it was. Neither of them can be reproved of defect when both did manifest a bold and knightly mind.

If it happens that one man should offend another in any way and he who is offended should lay a hand on his weapons and the other should fly, although the offended could not come to him, he who flies should be condemned for a wild man and a coward and the other should be honoured. Honour is seated in the face and hands, not in the shoulders and feet. To come to be made friends he should confess his baseness and ask forgiveness of his offence.

If one man should offend another not in any ill sort but wrongfully, and the other does not revenge himself being able to do it presently, the offender according to the quality of the person offended shall confess to have done wrong, or to have done it against reason, or such a thing as he ought not or not like a gentleman. In all these sorts yet he is to ask forgiveness of him.

If happily between maskers[*] (as often it happens) not knowing one another, one of them is injured, the amends should be to say: 'I knew you not and if I had known you I would not have done so unto you, but if I had done it I should have done discourteously, or villainously, or like a bad gentleman, asking pardon for it.' The same course is to be held when one man should offend another at night in the dark.

I will not omit that sometime a peace is made between men, which is not an agreement of the fact. For example, if I say that a

---

[*] One disguised who wears a visor.

man struck me and he denies that he touched me, in such case the satisfaction may be: 'I struck you not and if I did I did an ill deed', or suchlike words to this effect. By such similar examples other cases may likewise be ruled. To these and similar cases may be added those other words which are commonly used between knights, as we have accordingly made mention in the section 'Of satisfactions in general', above.

OF SATISFACTION TO BE MADE UPON INJURY BY WORD

It has been said before that the foundation of satisfactions does consist in the truth. To confirm the same, when a man has opposed against another any defect untruly, he ought to confess the matter is not as he said and may allege in excuse of himself (if the truth be not opposite against it) that he spoke it either thinking it to be so or because it was told him, or in choler. If he shall say that he thought so, he shall add that he was deceived or that he thought amiss and that he knows the truth to be otherwise. If he says it was told him, he shall say that he who told it to him said not the truth. If he says he spoke it in choler, he shall then say that he knows the truth to be otherwise, that he is sorry for it or discontented or grieved. In this sort all words spoken may be expressed and declared with a contrary sense. For example: 'I have called you traitor when I knew you to be an honourable and just knight', and, as often as there is demonstration that the truth is contrary to that spoken, he who is injured is discharged. If a man would not make mention of the injurious words, if he should revoke them in such sort as I have said, or with words of honourable witness the charge should nevertheless be taken away. If one man should give another the lie upon words of wrath he should also revoke it, but, if a man should make dainty to say I have belied you, he might in another sort yet honestly provide for it. He may say: 'I confess the words true spoken by you whereupon our quarrel is grown', or else he may express the very matter itself and allow it to be true.

I will not omit that seeking means to make quietness in controversies I have sometimes so handled a matter: I have made agreement by such a way that he who gave the lie has spoken to the other in this sort: 'I would be glad to know of you with what mind you gave me hard words the other day whereupon I gave you the lie. I pray you resolve me herein.'

The other has answered: 'To tell you the truth I spoke them in choler and not upon any other occasion.'

The first has replied:

> Since you have spoken those words in choler I assure you that I did not mean to have given you the lie unless you had spoken them with a deliberate mind to charge me. I say that my lie does not charge you but rather I acknowledge you for a man of truth and I pray you remember no discourteous words passed between us but hold me for your friend.

The other has answered: 'I do likewise judge you a man of honour beseeching you also to account me your friend.'

This form of satisfaction may be applied to a thousand cases that happen daily. By this example other forms and rules may be found according to the quality of the cases.

Moreover it does happen that when a man is grieved at another's ill words of him he denies that he spoke them. This some men question whether it should be taken for a full satisfaction. Some would have him say: 'I spoke them not, but if I had done it I had spoken falsely', or other like words of sense. Touching this doubt I think that if a man should speak ill of me, in denying to have spoken it he should greatly shame himself, but notwithstanding he should not give me satisfaction and yet he should be found to have wronged me. Therefore it is not sufficient only to deny, but a further matter is convenient.

If a man has not spoken ill he may recite all things, and if he has spoken it he ought to say something to satisfy the other. The words which he is to say are these: 'I have not spoken it, but if I had I should have spoken untrue', or 'committed that which I ought not, nor like a gentleman', or such like. But a gentleman should not be brought to deny that which he has spoken, but rather should confess it and make satisfaction if he should not deny it to be true. He should say that in speaking it he has offended him, that he should not have spoken it, or that he did ill and crave pardon for it. In all cases where an offence is it is requisite to ask pardon. A man may also offend in speaking the truth if his intent is to offend.

⋄⇌⇋⋄

THAT IT IS NO SHAME TO GIVE ANOTHER SATISFACTION

Forasmuch as we are to come ordinarily to satisfaction by way of denial (for so we will term revocations of words and confession to have done injuriously) some perhaps may say, if denial be so shameful (as you said before) as a man is infamed thereby and may be refelled in other quarrels by knights, how will you if I have spoken any false thing or done ill thing that I by denying should bring upon me such an infamy? Whereto although we have sufficiently answered before where we showed that a man should rather remove himself from error than continue in it obstinately, yet I affirm that there is a great difference between that which is done in the lists through force of Armes and that which is done abroad for love of the truth. One is forced and the other voluntary, one for fear of death, the other for right of reason. The one condemns a man for a bad knight who would fight against justice, and the to alter his resolution and to promise the prince to be friends with the Earl Rimondo to whom he went also and forced him in like manner to vow friendship to Lord Mathew.

The prince then having brought them both to consent to his purpose and demanded them to meet in his presence, where Lord Mathew (who had two very excellent proper gentlewomen to his daughters) being the elder spoke first and said: 'Count Rimondo, I am at peace with you and accept you for my friend and son and do give one of my daughters in marriage unto you with a hundred thousand crowns.' He accepted the conditions and so the peace was concluded to their great contention, the prince's great pleasure, and the joy of all his subjects without any more bloodshed or mortality.

A DANGEROUS SATISFACTION BETWEEN TWO GENTLEMEN, ONE CALLED THE BIANCHI AND THE OTHER NERI, WHEREOF ISSUED GREAT HARMS

I read in the history of Florence of two gentlemen in the city of Pistoia who were in very straight league of amity together. Having two sons, it happened the two youths kept company together. Once playing at cards they fell to words, and from words to blows. In the end one returned home to his father hurt. Understanding the whole matter, the father of the unhurt youth was very sorry that his friend's son was hurt by his. He rebuked his son bitterly and commanded him expressly upon his blessing to go to his friend the youth's father whom he had hurt and ask forgiveness for hurting his son.

Now, he seeing the youth and his son and not remembering or considering the great amity and friendship that was between himself and the youth's father caused his men to cut off his right hand, and so sent him back home again to his father saying that deeds could not be recompensed with words. This act and uncivil part caused great ruin and slaughter in Tuscany.

Therefore those who purpose to be reconciled and make peace, or go about to reconcile others and bring them in league, must take heed what they do and never trust to the discretion of him who is offended but see the conditions and points agreed upon first. If anyone do not keep his promise and do contrary to his faith and word passed they themselves who are the mediators and dealers in the making of the peace, as lovers of honour and justice, to be revenged of him, seeing such villainy and insolence worthily punished. For the most part such men are commonly the cause of their own overthrow, of their parents, friends and also of their country.

We read in histories of ancient times that a dying King of the Persians left two sons, each demanding the empire. While the matter was debated they conversed and lived together in all kindness and brotherly lovingness till it was declared by the peers of the empire which of them was chosen and elected to be the king. This the other took so well that he would not in any case be brought to think either unkindly of his brother or evil of the electors, he having what he aspired unto and they doing what they thought best and most convenient for the country. Such discretion would do well in all men to cut from them many inconveniences, debates, strifes and quarrels.

THE NOBILITY OF WOMEN

Having discoursed of the inequality in nobility, and especially of private noblemen and gentlemen, I will not take occasion now to say anything of the means and manner whereby men rise unto honour and dignity, nor of the greatness and nobility of kingdoms, provinces and cities, considering that this matter has been so largely and laudably handled by many as appears by reading the ancient and modern histories which are filled with discourses tending to this purpose.

Only this I will say by the way that those places have been famed most noble and had in greatest account, which have produced bravest men commended unto posterity for their virtue – either intellectual or active, moral or politick, civil or military. As places are made famous or ennobled by reason of the excellent men who are born there, so also can no place how barbarous it be drown or darken the glory and commendation due unto a man ennobled by valour, prudence or other virtues whatsoever. As Anacharsis, being noted by one to be a Scythian, answered as sharply as readily, true indeed by birth but not by bringing up. He was a Scythian born, yet his manners were not barbarous nor his life Scythian like but deserved the commendation due to civil and virtuous education.

I will leave the virtues and nobilities of men and turn my speech to women, hoping they will not be offended by me if I discover the virtues and noble disposition of their sex. This being such as deserves highest commendation, I utterly disallow the opinion that not only does not attribute nobility unto women but also abridges them from power and ability to ennoble and import nobility unto others. In diverse histories we read of many excellent women both of high and low estate, whose excellence has been carried throughout the world for rare virtue. Some are for valour, others for learning, others for wisdom, others for chastity, others for other singular virtues and commendable parts. Many queens and noble ladies have gotten great renown and become glorious for Armes and war-like exploits. Many have had their names dedicated to everlasting remembrance even by the memorial of their own pens, having been most exquisite writers and penwomen themselves for prose and verse both.

In my opinion then women are greatly wronged by them who seem to take from them power of transferring nobility to others, excluding them from so great an honour, they notwithstanding having great reason to be copartners with men therein. Excellency consists in virtue of the body and the mind. Women being endowed with both beauty and virtue and seeing that women can learn whatsoever men can, having the full use of reason or else nature (who does never do anything in vain) should have to no purpose given them the gift of understanding. I think they deserve fellowship and communing in honour with men considering nature has bestowed on them as well as on men a means to attain learning, wisdom and all other virtues active and contemplative. This is made manifest by the example of many who have confirmed the opinion of their valour and excellency by their rare virtue and almost incredible prowess.

To recite the worthy acts of some I will wholly commit and pass by the Amazons, their story being counted fabulous, and mention

The Nobility of Women

some whose valiant and virtuous acts have been recorded in true histories of old times as well as our times. The king Argus having want of men by reason of long-continued great wars, Theselide a woman of a city wherein Argus was besieged by Cleomenes, King of Lacedemony, provoked the other women in the city to take Armes. Leading them out at the gates she delivered the city from siege and put their enemies to shameful flight. I will not hear speak of the valour of Artemisia, Isicrate, Semiramis, Tomiris, the women of Lacedemony, Debora, Judith and others virtuous and magnanimous, yea holy and sacred ladies whose histories are contained in the holy Scripture. I will come unto those whose life was not so long since that we may well remember them.

About the time that the Englishmen had brought in subjection the greatest part of that kingdom under Charles VI there was a young maiden called Jane Pulzela, daughter to a shepherd of the Duke of Loraine. Not yet reaching the fifteenth year of her age she was accounted to be a prophetess and many held her to be a witch, but this makes not to the purpose. Being in great doubt of his fortune the King sent for her to find out whether or not he should lose the rest of his kingdom. Having answered that he should become victorious in the end, he gave the more credit unto it, because many of his noblemen assured him that she had the spirit of prophecy, recounting many things to him which she had declared in private men's estates. Afterward she took Armes herself and behaved in such sort among the other captains and men of Armes that in a very short time she was made captain general of the whole army. Being armed and mounted on a barbed horse in such sort as she was not known but to be a man she made a sally with all her troops, both horse and foot. Assailing the enemy with an undaunted courage she followed her enterprise with such valour and prudence that she freed the city of Orleans from the siege, being herself shot through the shoulder with an arrow. Thence she led her company to Troyes in Campain, where being encamped against the expectation of all the captains and soldiers, they took the city in very short time and caused Charles VII to be crowned in Reims as the ancient custom is, having first delivered the city from the siege which the enemy had laid unto it. Shortly after battering Paris and clambering on the walls as being famous among the stoutest soldiers, notwithstanding her leg was pierced quite through with an arrow, gave not over the enterprise for all that but persisted till she had effected it.

Petrarch writes that he knew a damsel at Pozzuelo called Marie who borrowing the habit of a young man, after the fashion men wore their apparel there, armed herself. She was the first who fought with the enemy and the last to retire.[*]

Ursina, wife unto Guido the chief of the house of Torrello, understanding the Venetians had laid siege to Guastella a castle of her husband's, but he being abroad, armed herself and led a company of men to the defended castle and spoiled many Venetians.

Margaret, daughter to Valdiner King of Suetia and wife to Aquinus King of Norway, remained inheritress unto those kingdoms in the right of her husband, her father and her son, Olaus also of Dacia. The Duke of Monopoli waged war against her, but she encountered him with a mighty army and defeated his forces, took him prisoner and led him in her triumph after the solemn order of the Romans.

Mahomet, King of the Turks, waging war against the Venetians sent a great army under the conduct of one of his general captains to take the Isle of Metelino and besieging Coccino very strongly the inhabitants issued and fought very valiantly against the Turks. In the same city was a young maid who, seeing her father slain by the Turks in this fight and the citizens beginning to faint and fear,

---

[*] From Petrarch's letter to Cardinal Giovanni Colonna of 23 November 1343, in Catherine Moriarty (ed.), *The Voice of the Middle Ages in Personal Letters 1100–1500*, Book V, letter 4 as titled by Aldo S. Bernardo; http://www.petrarch.petersadlon.com/letters_list.html (accessed August 2013).

got into the former companies and skirmished so courageously with the Turks that all the citizens were ashamed to see themselves overcome in stoutness and courage by a simple girl so they took heart and utterly destroyed their enemies to save the city.

Bona Lombarda, first servant and afterward wife to Petro Brunoro of Parma, being in the wars that the Venetians had against Francesco Sforza Duke of Milan,* after Pauono a castle in the territories of Brescia was taken, with her courage and gallant forwardness recovered it again.

Margaret, wife to Henry, King of England, and sister to Renatus, King of Naples, being informed that her husband was overcome in battle and taken prisoner, presently gathered certain companies together and led them to a place where the enemy was to pass, encountered them, overcame their camp and pursued those who fled with her husband the king. She slew an infinite company of men and in the end saved him, returned home with him and got him this most glorious victory.

I remember when I was a youth, a friend of mine, son to a trumpet in pay under the captains of the Signorie of Venice, was with a certain cousin set upon by eleven other young men who were their enemies. His mother perceiving this took a partisan in her hands and defended her son and cousin, sorely wounded five of their enemies and made the rest fly.

Being in Ravenna I saw in one of the churches the carved image of a lady who, being wife to a gentleman who was chief of the house of Rasponi, had ever in her lifetime accompanied her husband in all his wars and achieved immortal fame by her prowess and valour.

I was in Lombard on a day which was generally solemnised according to the custom over the whole country. It happened at that time that there was a great quarrel between two rich houses among the farmers and countrymen of that place. The one part

---

* Francesco II Sforza was Duke of Milan from 1521 to 1535.

was called the Romani and the other the Ferrarisi. Both being under the Duke of Ferrara and meeting on the universal feast day at a village called Tresenta, one of the Romani shot a pistol at the chief of the Ferrarisi and, thinking to have wounded him, missed him and hurt one of the Ferrarisi's wives. She was of so valiant a disposition that, although she was shot quite through, she said nothing to her friends, nor complained of it, lest they should have left their enemies and come to help her. Many of them might have in the meanwhile been spoiled by the adverse part. Snatching a weapon out of one of her countrymen's hands she slew him who had shot her and his fellow who fought by him and then fell down not able to perform anymore, living but four days after.

I have read in the chronicles of France that two great men grew to be enemies for the dukedom of Bretagne – the one pretending an estate in right of his father as his by inheritance, the other claiming interest in it by the right of his wife as her dowry, etc. One of them was much favoured by the King of France and the other of the King of England. These two rising up in arms, the one whom the king there least favoured was taken and put in prison, and the Frenchmen began to spoil his country, take his tenants, and coming to a city where the lady was, wife to him that was taken, besieged it and often assailed it in vain. Like a right valiant gentlewoman and of a manly courage she provided that not one woman in the city should be idle, but bring her helping hand for the defence of the city and maintenance of their honour, causing some to make instruments of pitch and tar and fireworks, others to bring stones, seething water and other thing necessary at that instant. Many times she issued very valorously and bravely, firing her enemy's tents. She put them to great loss and confusion, slaying many of them, but they daily received new supplies from the king, and she was forced to send for some succour to the King of England. While she waited they drove her to many inconveniences. The people began to mutter and to mutiny within the city, finding

The Nobility of Women

great want and scarcity, by reason whereof many died. She was much solicited and importuned to deliver up the city to the enemy. Not knowing how to answer them she desired them to stay for God's mercy, just so many days (limiting a certain time) and if no aid came in the meanwhile then she would do their request. Those days being expired, while she was heavily musing what answer to make her citizens who had very earnestly besought her again to render, spied the English navy on the seas and calling them to her window, comforted them with that sight. She caused all things to be prepared and made in a readiness so that when her English friends landed and should assault the enemy she might make a sally to meet them with her companies and bid them welcome to the destruction and utter overthrow of her enemies. This she did and slew so many of the Frenchmen that all the country was amazed thereat and she maintained wars against them a long time after.

I have read in the histories of the Turks, how Selim Sultan obtained the empire after he had poisoned his father and strangled his brother Corcut, who was a philosopher. With a mighty army he pursued his brother Accomat, whom the King of Persia, Usan Cassano, much favoured and helped with men, provision and money. The brothers meeting together and the victory being very doubtful for a great while, in the end Selim Sultan overcame by the valour of his janissaries.* The Persians, having with their horses broken quite through the whole battle and entered on the janissaries in the midst of whom the Turk Selim Sultan was guarded, discharged a volley of shot upon the Persians who were unused to hearing such a noise. They were wonderfully dismayed and instantly forced to take flight. By this means Sultan Selim obtained a wonderful great victory, and his brother Accomat was strangled by his janissaries. After the fight was done they found among those who were taken and dead an infinite company of

---

* An elite military unit of the Turkish army started in the fourteenth century.

Persian gentlewomen who had come all armed as knights to fight with their husbands. Selim Sultan caused the dead to be solemnly buried and those who were saved to be sent home to their countries very honourably.

In 1571 Selim, emperor of the Turks and father to Amurat who now lives, waged war against the Venetians. Grand Vizier Bassa[*] travelled by sea to the city Raguzi in the Isle of Carsola and began to batter it. The citizens perceiving and fearing the danger fled with their goods and such things as they made most account of into the isle and left none but women at home. They chose to die rather than fall into the Turks' hands and went valiantly to the walls. One of them putting fire to the piece of ordinance stroke away with the bullet the lantern of Bassa whereupon he hoisted sail and fled and thus the city was saved.

In the time of Charles V and Francis, King of France, they having soldiers in Italy by reason of the dissention and factions among the Italians, the city of Siena was besieged. A gentlewoman of the house of Piccolomini was made colonel of the three thousand other women and achieved wonderful matters to the astonishment of all the people.

I have been told by diverse people of a Portuguese gentlewoman who about four years now ago left the apparel of her sex and went into Barbary as a soldier for religion's sake. She behaved herself so resolutely that she was made a captain in short time and became very famous, fearful to her enemies and greatly esteemed of her friends. In the end she chanced to go to confession and betrayed her sex to her confessor, who told her that it was a great sin to delude the world in taking upon her the person of a man and she could not do this without offending God. Besides this, he told the bishop of it, and the whole matter was known through the country where she was. Whereupon diverse noblemen, knowing her to be

---

[*] See footnote on p. 58 for more details.

a woman, desired to be married unto her, but she refused them because she loved a nephew of the bishop's and conversed with him very privately before she was known. Being discovered, she would not marry anyone but him for she would admit none to the near point of acquaintance as he was except him who should be her husband, being of as good a disposition that way as she was in matters of valour and courage. She was seen afterward in Lisbon apparelled like a woman, but armed like a knight leading a troop of men, the conduction of which she had obtained for her husband.

It was an infinite work for me to recite all the famous ladies who have been renowned for their virtue. Neither is it possible for any man to truly make a collection of all their gallant deeds, seeing they are so exceeding in number. As I have mentioned and called to remembrance some who were excelling in magnanimity, courage and greatness of the mind, so now I will also set down the names of some who passed in greatness of understanding and excelled in intellectual virtues.

Saffo of Lesbos was inferior to few poets in that art and superior to many. Erinna wrote a poem in the Doric tongue, which compared to Homer's divine work. Corina put down that great poet Pindarus five times. Pythagoras learned many things of his sister Themistoclea, and his daughter Dama was so excellent in learned mysteries that she commented and expounded the difficult places in her father's works. Areta of Cirena, after the death of her father Aristippus, kept the school while she lived and read philosophy, lectured daily and wonderfully increased the audience. Leontia wrote against Theophrastus, Aristotle's scholar. Hipatia was very skilful in astronomy and professed it publicly a long time in Alexandria.

To leave the Grecian gentlewomen and come to the Italian. Sempronia of Rome was excellently well spoken both in Greek and Latin. She was a fine poet and wrote very sweetly. Cornelia Africanus' wife was nothing inferior unto the former. Nor

Hortensia, who was in verity her father's true heir in eloquence and oratory. Sulpicia, Roman lady, in heroical verse deplored the pitiful time of Domitian the emperor. In our times we have heard of Russuida of Saxony, who was excellent in the tongues and has written diverse treatises and poems very commendably. Batista, eldest daughter to Galeazo, Lord of Pessaro, made many excellent proofs of her learning and wrote many pamphlets. In the same city of Pessaro was a gentlewoman called Laura Brenzara, who has written many verses in both Latin and Italian. She was admired for her excellency in making orations and extemporal speeches in both tongues, Latin and Italian. At Padua where I was born, in my time was a gentlewoman of good reckoning who professed the civil law publicly. She came daily into the colleges and schools and disputed with all the doctors and scholars of the university. Cassandra, a gentlewoman of Venice, was commended for great skill in languages and spoke very eloquently. She could also write very well as appeared by diverse books she has set forth, among which has been known a book of the order of the sciences.

I will content myself, having produced these examples in proof of the valour and virtue of women, by concluding with only one more, which as the best I kept to be last. Herein I imitate the best orators, who always reserve the strongest arguments for last. These lines therefore shall be adorned and honoured with the name of this most glorious Princess Elizabeth, our gracious queen, whose fame has built her towers of triumphs even in countries farthest removed from her and forced her very enemies in the storm of their malice and spite to praise her name, to admire her mercifulness and wisdom, and to fear her power. This is such a manifest and worthy example of womanly worthiness and feminine perfection that the most perfect men must by truth's enforcement acknowledge themselves most unperfect in regard of the meanest perfection that heaven has most bountifully bestowed on her sacred majesty, who lives yet renowned through the whole world, the Son of

Christendom, and the only star whereby all people are directed to the place which abounds in peace, religion and virtue. She is a princess truly accomplished with all virtue both moral and intellectual, with greatness both of mind and understanding and with heavenly wisdom to govern royally both in peace and wars, to the credit and glory of all her sex. God of his mercy maintain her life in much prosperity, even a whole eternity that, as her virtue is heavenly and immortal, so she herself may never die, but when the world and all must perish be carried up to heaven by holy angels, there to live in God's eternal glory.

FINIS

Appendices

Appendix A

A Transcription of the Section on Saviolo in Florio, *Second Frutes*

p. 117:

G. But to come to our purpose againe, of whome doo you learne to plaie at your weapon?
E. Of master V. S.
G. Who, that Italian that lookes like Mars himselfe.
E. The verie same.
G. Where dwels he?
E. In the little striate, where the well is.
G. Alas we have a great waie thether yet.
E. Pardon me sir, it is but hard by.
G. At what signe dwels he?
E. At the signe of the red Lyon.
G. Dooth he plaie well? Hath he good skill in his weapon?
E. As much as any other man.
G. Is he valiant, and a talle man of his hands?
E. More valiant than a sword it selfe.
G. How much doo you give him a moneth?
E. I have made no price with him.
G. What weapon doo you plaie at moste?
E. At rapier and dagger, or rapier and cloake.
G. The true and right gentleman-like weapons.
E. Truelie he teacheth verie well, and verie quicklie.

G. Have you learned to give a thrust?
E. Yea, and to warde it also, and I know all the advantages, how a man must charge and enter upon his enemie.
G. You have spent your time verie well then.
E. I cannot tell what I shoulde doo else.

p. 119:

G. What place in Italie was he borne in?
E. I take him to be a Padoan.
G. I have heard him reported to be a notable talle man.
E. Hee will hit any man, bee it with a thrust or stoccada, with an imbroccada or a charging blowe, with a right or reverse blowe, be it with the edge, with the back, or with the flat, even as it liketh him.
G. Is he left or right handed?
E. Both, all is one to him.
G. What dooth he commonlie take a moneth.
E. But, little, and there is no man that teacheth with more dextereritie and nimbleness than he.
G. Can he doo nothing else, but plaie at fence?
E. Yes, hee hath good skill in everie kinde of weapon, hee shootes well in a peece, he shootes weill in great ordinance, and besides he is a verie excellent good souldier.
G. All these rare good qualities doo verie seeldome times, concur in anie one of our fencers.
E. Moreover, hee is a good dancer, hee danceth verie well, both galiards, and pauins, hee vaultes most nimblie, and capers verie loftilie.
G. He differs verie much from other fencers.
E. Yet there are manie honest and proper men among them.

G. There be some, but one swallowe brings not sommer, nor one divell makes not hell.
E. Is he a great quarelour, and a brauler?
G. He is most patient, nether dooth he goe about to revenge any injurie that is offered him, unless it touch his credit and honour verie far.

Appendix B

A Transcription of the Section on Saviolo in Silver, *Paradoxes of Defence*

Then came Vincentio and Jeronimo, they taught rapier fight at the court, at London, and in the country, by the space of seven or eight years or thereabouts. These two Italian fencers, especially Vincentio, said Englishmen were strong men, but had no cunning, and they would go back too much in their fight, which was great disgrace unto them. Upon these words of disgrace against Englishmen, my brother Toby Silver and myself, made challenge against them both, to play with them at the single rapier, rapier and dagger, the single dagger, the single sword, the sword and target, the sword and buckler, & two hand sword, the staff, battle axe, and Morris pike, to be played at the Bell Savage upon the scaffold, where he that went in his fight faster back than he ought, of Englishmen or Italian, should be in danger to break his neck off the scaffold. We caused to that effect, five or six score bills of challenge to be printed, and set up from Southwarke to the Tower, and from thence throughout London unto Westminster, we were at the place with all these weapons at the time appointed, within a bow shot of their fence school. Many gentlemen of good account, carried many of the bills of challenge unto them, telling them that now the Silvers were at the place appointed, with all their weapons, looking for them, and a multitude of people there to behold the fight, saying unto them, now come and go with us (you shall take no wrong) or else you are shamed for ever. Do the gentlemen what they could, these gallants would not come to the place of trial. I verily think their cowardly fear to answer this challenge, had utterly shamed them indeed, had not the masters of Defence of London, within two or three days after, been drinking of bottled ale hard by Vincentio's school, in a hall where the Italians must of necessity pass through to go to their school, and as they were coming by, the masters of defence did pray them to drink with them. But the Italians being very cowardly, were afraid, and presently drew their rapiers. There was a pretty wench standing by, that loved the Italians. She ran with outcry into the street: 'Help! Help! The Italians are like to be slain.' The people with all speed came running into the house, and with their capes and such things as they could, parted the fray, for the English masters of defence, meant nothing less than to soil their hands upon these two faint hearted fellows. The next morning after, all the court was filled, that the Italian teachers of fence had beaten all the masters of defence in London, who set upon them in a house together. This won the Italian fencers their credit again, and thereby got much, still continuing their false teaching to the end of their lives.

The Vincentio proved himself a stout man not long before he died, that it might be seen in his lifetime he had been a gallant, and therefore no marvel he took upon him so highly to teach Englishmen to fight, and to set forth books of the feats of arms. Upon a time at Wels in Somersetshire, as he was in great bravery among the many gentlemen of good account, with great boldness he gave out speeches, that he had been thus many years in England, and since the time of his first coming, there was not yet one Englishman, that could touch him at the single rapier, or the rapier and dagger. A valiant gentleman being there among the rest, his English heart did rise to hear this proud boaster, secretly sent a messenger to one Bartholomew Bramble, a friend of his, a very tall man of both his hands and person, who kept a school of defence in

Appendix B

the town. The messenger by the way made the master of defence acquainted with the mind of the gentleman that sent for him, and of all what Vincentio had said. This master of defence presently came, and among all the gentlemen with his cap off, prayed master Vincentio, that he would be pleased to take a quart of wine with him. Vincentio very scornfully looking upon him, said unto him: 'Wherefore should you give me a quart of wine?' 'Merry sir', said he, 'because I hear you are a famous man at your weapon.' Then presently said the gentleman that sent for the master of defence: 'He is a man of your profession.' 'My profession?' said Vincentio, 'what is my profession?' Then said the the gentleman: 'He is a master of the noble science of defence.' 'Why', said Vincentio, 'God made him a good man.' But the master of defence would not thus leave him, but prayed him again he would be pleased to take a quart of wine of him. Then said Vincentio: 'I have no need of your wine.' Then said the master of defence: 'Sir I have a school of defence in the town, will it please you to go thither?' 'Your school?' said master Vincentio. 'What shall I do at your school?' 'Play with me [said the master] at the rapier and dagger, if it please you.' 'Play with you?' said master Vincentio. 'If I play with you, I will hit you 1, 2, 3, 4 thrusts in the eye together.' Then said the master of defence: 'If you can do so, it is the better for you, and the worse for me, but surely I can hardly believe that you can hit me. But yet once again I heartily pray you good sir, that you will go to my school and play with me.' 'Play with you?' said master Vincentio (very scornfully), 'by God let me scorn to play with you.' With the word scorn, the master of defence was very much moved, and up with his great English fist, and struck master Vincentio such a box on the ear that he fell over and over, his legs just against a buttery hatch, whereon stood a great black jack. The master of defence fearing the worst, against Vincentio his rising, caught the black jack into his hand, being more than half full of beer. Vincentio lustily started up, laying his hand upon his dagger, & with the other hand pointed with his finger,

Appendix B

saying, very well: 'I will cause to lie in the Gaile for this geare[?], 1, 2, 3, 4 years.' And well said the master of defence: 'Since you will drink no wine, will you pledge me in beer? I drink to all cowardly knaves in England, and I think you to be the very most coward of them all.' With that he cast all the beer upon him, notwithstanding Vincentio having nothing but his gilt rapier, and dagger about him, and the other for his defence the black jack, would not at that time fight it out: but the next day met with the master of defence in the street, and said unto him: 'You remember how misused a me yesterday, you were to blame, me being an excellent man, me teach you to thrust two feet further than any Englishman, but first come you with me.' Then he brought him to a mercers shop, and said to the mercer: 'Let me see your best silken points.' The mercer then did presently show him some of seven groats a dozen. Then he paid fourteen groats for two dozen, and said to the master of defence: 'There is one dozen for you, and one dozen for me.' This was one of the valiant fencers that came from beyond the seas, to teach Englishmen how to fight, and this was one of the many frays, that I have heard of, that ever he made in England, wherein he showed himself a far better man in his life, than in his profession he was. For he professed arms, but in his life a better Christian. He set forth in print a book for the use of the rapier and dagger, the which he called *His Practise*, I have read it over, and because I find therein neither true rule for the perfect teaching of the true fight, nor true ground of the true fight, neither sense nor reason for due proof thereof. I have thought it frivolous to recite any part therein contained: yet that the truth thereof may appear, let two men being well experienced in the rapier and dagger fight, choose any of the best branches in the same book, & make trial with force and agility, without which the truth between the true & false fight cannot be known, & they shall find great imperfections therein. And again, for proof that there is no truth, neither in his rules, grounds or rapier fight, let trial be made in this manner. Set two unskillful men together at the rapier and dagger, being valiant, and you shall see, that once in two bouts there shall either one or both of them be hurt. Then set two skillful men together, being valiant at the rapier and dagger, and they shall do the like. Then set a skillful rapier and dagger man, the best that can be had, and valiant man having no skill together at rapier & dagger, and once in two bouts upon my credit in all the experience I have in fight, the unskillful man, do the other what he can for his life for the contrary, shall hurt him, and most commonly if it were in continuance of fight, you shall see the unskillful man to have the advantage. And if I should choose a valiant man for service of the prince, or to take part with me or any friend of mine in a good quarrel, I would chose the unskillful man, because unencumbered with false fights, because such a man stands free in his valour with strength and agility of body, freely takes the benefit of nature, fights most brave, by losing no opportunity, either soundly to hurt his enemy, or defend himself. But the other standing for his defence, upon cunning Italian wards, Punta reversa, the Imbrocata, Stocata, and being fast tied unto these false fights, stands troubled in his wits, and nature thereby racked through the largeness or false lyings or spaces, whereby he is in his fight as a man half maimed, losing the opportunity of times and benefit of nature, & whereas before being ignorant of these false rapier fights, standing in the free liberty of nature given to him by God, he was able in the field with his weapons to answer the most valiant man in the world, but now being tied unto that false, fickle uncertain fight, thereby has lost in nature his freedom, is now become scarce half a man, and every boy in that fight is become as good a man as himself [. . .]

Jeronimo presently went forth of the coach and drew his rapier and dagger, put himself into his best ward or Stocata, which ward was taught by himself and Vincentio, and by them best allowed of, to be the best ward to stand upon in fight for life, either to assault the enemy, or stand and watch his coming, which ward it should seem he ventured his life upon, but howsoever with all the fine Italianated skill Jeronimo had, Cheese with his sword within two thrusts ran him into the body and slew him. Yet the Italian teachers will say, that an Englishman cannot thrust straight with a sword, because the hilt will not suffer him to put the forefinger upon the blade, nor to hold the pommel in the hand, whereby we are of necessity to hold fast the handle in the hand. By reason whereof we are driven to thrust both compass and short, whereas with the rapier they can thrust both straight and much further than we can with the sword, because of the hilt. And these are the reasons they make against the sword.

Bibliography

Anglin, J. P., 'The Schools of Defence in Elizabethan London', *Renaissance Quarterly*, Vol. 37, No. 3 (Autumn 1984).

Anon. [attributed to William Segar, but probably by Vincentio Saviolo], *The Book of Honour & Armes*, London, Richard Jones, 1590.

Aylward, J. D., *The English Master of Arms*, London, Routledge & Kegan Paul, 1956.

Berry, H., *The Noble Science: A Study and Transcription of Sloane Ms. 2530*, London, Associated University Presses, 1991.

Blount, T., *Glossographia Anglicana Nova: Or, A Dictionary, Interpreting Such Hard Words of Whatever Language, as are at Present Used in the English Tongue, with Their Etymologies, Definition, &c. Also the Terms of Divinity, Law, Physick, Mathematicks, History, Agriculture, Logick, Metaphysicks, Grammar, Poetry, Musick, Heraldry, Architecture, Painting, War, and All Other Arts and Sciences are Herein Explain'd . . .*, London, D. Brown, 1707.

Bullen, A. H. (ed.), *The Works of John Marston*, Vol. III *The Scourge of Villainy*, London, Ballantyne Press, 1887.

Carr, R. (trans.), *The Mahumetane or Turkish Historie Containing Three Bookes: 1 Of the Originall and Beginning of the Turkes, and of the Foure Empires Which are Issued and Proceded Out of the Superstitious Sect of Mahumet . . .*, London, printed by Thomas Este, 1600.

Chatfield, C., 'Stranger 929', 2010; http://www.the1595.com/documents/STRANGER-929.pdf (accessed August 2013).

Cotgrave, R., *A Dictionarie of the French and English Tongues*, London, Adam Islip, 1611.

Crollalanza, G. B. di, *Dizionario Storico-Blasonico delle famiglie nobili e notabili Italiane estinte e fiorenti compilato dal commendatore G.B. di Crollalanza,* Vol. 2 L–S, Pisa, Pisa Presso la direzione del giornale Araldico, 1888.

Drew, F., *The Lombard Laws*, Philadelphia, University of Pennsylvania Press, 1973.

Florio, J., *Florios Second Frutes, to be Gathered of Twelve Trees, of Divers but Delightsome Tastes to the Tongues of Italians and Englishmen. To Which is Annexed his Gardine of Recreation Yeelding Six Thousand Italian Proverbs*, London, Thomas Woodcock, 1591.

Florio, J., *A Worlde of Wordes, or Most Copious, and Exact Dictionarie in Italian and English, Collected by John Florio*, London, Edw. Blount, 1598.

Gifford, W., *The Works of Ben Jonson*, London, Warne & Routledge, 1860.

Greene, R., *Greenes Groats-worth of Witte, Bought with a Million of Repentance*, New York, Burt Franklin, 1970.

Hardy, R., *Longbow: A Social and Military History*, Cambridge, Stephens, 1976.

Harrison, W., *The Description of England: The Classic Contemporary Account of Tudor Social Life by William Harrison*, edited by Georges Edelen, New York, Dover, 1994.

Haynes, A., 'Italian Immigrants to England, 1550–1603', *History Today*, Vol. 27 (August 1977).

Holmer, J. O., 'Draw if You be Men', *Shakespeare Quarterly*, Vol. 45, No. 2 (1994).

Jackson, J. L., *Three Elizabethan Fencing Manuals*, reprinted by Scholars' Facsimiles & Reprints, Ann Arbor, MI, 2001.

Kelso, R., 'Saviolo and His Practise', *Modern Language Notes*, Vol. 39, No. 1 (January 1924).

Touching the Satisfaction that Ought to be Made Between Knights

other shows that a man will do anything rather than take weapons in injustice. One shows that he who has once undertaken to defend an ill quarrel is like to do it another time. The other gives testimony that renouncing the quarrel, not to fight wrongfully, he will not be brought to take weapons except for a just and lawful occasion. In sum, as one is the part of a bad knight and disloyal, so the other is the testimony of sincerity and true faithfulness. Seeing that no man lives without sin, he is more to be commended among men having committed any error and knowing it forthwith repents and seeks to make true satisfaction. A knight who acknowledging his fault and seeks to amend it does not only deserve no blame but is worthy of much commendation. He is like a man governing himself by reason, like a knight takes justice for his guide and like a Christian observes the true law.

For these reasons then all knights ought to embrace it and all princes to esteem it highly, both the one and the other accounting no less the faith and purity of the mind than the pride and bodily strength. Forasmuch as strength is as profitable to mankind as it is governed by reason and integrity, only itself suffices to govern innumerable multitudes in peace. Force that is not accompanied with ripe counsel is that with which the ruin of nations overturns all divine and humane laws. Because I know the vulgar sort account satisfaction baseness I will thereto answer no other, but that the choosing rather to fight wrongfully than satisfy by reason is judged beastliness of every man of understanding.

Of Honour & Honourable Quarrels

SATISFACTION DONE TO ONE IN BURGUNDY, BY DEATH FOR HIS INSOLENCE

A certain quarrel rose between two soldiers who I knew very well – one, a Normand of Roan called James Luketo, a man very well experienced in Armes, who falling into some words with the other (being at Geneva) gave him a box on the ear. Whereupon he answered Luketo that, because he knew Luketo to have great skill in his weapon which he had not, but being a soldier would fight and challenged Luketo to meet him with his piece. He went to the general of the army and obtained leave for the open field with his consent and the other commanders who were present at the action.

Seeing that many discharges passed between them yet neither took any hurt, the general suffered them to charge their pieces no more but sought to reconcile them again and make them friends. Both parties agreed that he of Geneva to whom the box on the ear was given by Luketo should in the presence of the general and other captains of the army strike Luketo on the shoulder and say: 'I am satisfied, we will be friends.'

But the soldier of Geneva, being of a stout stomach when he came to do as it was concluded, took Luketo a sound blow on the ear. Taking this for a great injury being in that presence and against the order set down, Luketo drew his sword presently and ran him through slaying him out of hand, justly rewarding him for his insolence.

Sure I think it was the just judgement of God, who uses to show his justice upon them that are so insolent and full of contumacy* and envious malice that regarding neither what they pass their words for privately among themselves, nor the intercession of noble gentlemen and worthy personages, who seek their safety and

---

* See footnote on p. 95

welfare, care for nothing but the fulfilling of their headiness and revenging appetite.

My opinion concerning these reconciliations is that it was not good in the making of them to allow any sign of revenge to pass between the parties that are to be reconciled. If satisfaction in the treating of any peace between two fallen out can be made by words, I think it would not be amiss if all tokens or signs of revenge were avoided.

SATISFACTION UNTO ONE WHO WAS TREACHEROUSLY HURT

I made mention above (upon occasion) of two captains called Montarno and Faro, the beginning of their quarrel you heard before. The end was such. Montarno being ungently and cowardly hurt accused Faro of having dealt with him not like a man, which Faro denied. The matter could not be taken up between them, although many gentlemen travailed in it. They appointed to meet one another having each of them a godfather (as they call him) appointed to him. Whereupon the godfather who was to go with Faro, being wise, circumspect and a very honest man besides, said unto him when he was going to encounter Montarno: 'Look what you do, for you go to a place where God overthrows the strongest and gives the victory to the weakest if he fight justly. Therefore if you have offended Montarno make him satisfaction.' Whereunto Faro answered: 'Why, what satisfaction will Montarno have?' Whereupon it was agreed that Faro should confess that he esteemed Montarno a brave gentleman and honourable soldier and that while he did unbutton his doublet he meant not to offer him injury however it fell out and therefore would gladly have him to be his friend. Thus the peace was made up between them, but I think it a folly for men to trust their enemies having their weapons ready in their hands to injury or wrong them.

<hr>

A PEACE MADE BETWEEN TWO NOBLEMEN, BY THE ARCHDUKE CHARLES, SON TO THE EMPEROR MAXIMILIAN

There were two noblemen of account under Archduke Charles, prince of Stiria, Carinthia and some places in Croatia and of Friuli, who were both of the confines of Friuli. One of them was called the Earl Rimondo of Torre, with whom I have served in wars when he was colonel of certain companies of the emperor's in Croatia against the Turks. At this time the Christians had as famous a victory as likely has been heard of, by the industry and valorous virtue of General Pernome and the lord Firinbergher.

To return to our purpose, the other nobleman was called Lord Mathew Ouuer. They both being in mortal enmity, one incensed against the other which was cause of much bloodshed and the death of many fine gentlemen and knights. The Archduke Charles, their prince, perceiving this to be a lamentable thing caused both noblemen to be called to the court and placing them into sundry lodgings about himself (desirous of his subjects' welfare) separately went to each, first to Rimondo, dissuading him from his hostile mind and hatred towards Lord Mathew.

Finding him very obstinate and altogether resisting all peace and agreement, found he could not be reconciled with honour and would rather die than make a peace ignominious unto him. Whereupon the Archduke replied that if he were resolved rather to die than to yield to his entreaty he should be resolved and look to himself for he should die in deed. With that he called for an officer criminal to execute him presently. This soon moved Lord Mathew

Bibliography

Lillywhite, B., *London Signs: A Reference Book of London Signs from Earliest Times to About the Mid-Nineteenth Century, etc.*, London, George Allen & Unwin, 1972.

Livius, T., *History of Rome*, Vol. 1; available at http://etext.virginia.edu/etcbin/toccer-new2?id=Liv1His.sgm&images=images/modeng&data=/texts/english/modeng/parsed&tag=public&part=teiHeader (accessed August 2013).

Lodge, T., 'Wits Miserie, and the Worlds Madnesse: Discouering the Deuils Incarnat of this Age', *The Complete Works of Thomas Lodge*, 4 vols, 1883; reprint New York, Russell & Russell, 1963, Vol. 4.

Matthey, C. G. R. (ed.), *The Works of George Silver: Comprising 'Paradoxes of Defence' and 'Bref Instructions upon my Paradoxes of Defence'*, London: George Bell, 1898.

McCollum, L., 'Dispelling Myths about the Early History of Rapier Fencing in England', *Spada II: An Anthology of Swordsmanship*, Highland Village, TX, The Chivalry Bookshelf, 2005.

McElroy, M. and Cartwright, K., 'Public Fencing Contests on the Elizabethan Stage', *Journal of Sport History*, Vol. 13, No. 3 (Winter 1986).

Miller, W. (trans.), *De Officiis XIII, Marcus Tullius Cicero*, Loeb edn, Cambridge, MA, Harvard University Press, 1913.

Moriarty, C., (ed.), *The Voice of the Middle Ages in Personal Letters 1100–1500*, Book V, letter 4 as titled by Aldo S. Bernardo; http://www.petrarch.petersadlon.com/letters_list.html (accessed August 2013).

Morsberger, R. E., *Swordplay and the Elizabethan and Jacobean Stage*, Salzburg, Universität Salzburg, Institut für Englische Sprache und Literatur, 1974.

Muzio, G., *Il Duello del Mutio Iustinopolitano*, Vinegia, Gabriel Giolito de Ferrari e fratelli, 1550.

Palsgrave, J., *Lesclaircissement de la Langue Francoyse*, London, Johan Haukyns, 1530.

Bibliography

Perceval, R., *A Dictionarie in Spanish and English, first Published into the English Tongue by Ric. Percivale Gent, 1591, Now Enlarged and Amplified . . . by John Minsheu*, London, Edm. Bollifant, 1599.

Saviolo, V., *His Practise in Two Books, The First, Intreating of the Use of the Rapier and Dagger; The Second, Of Honour & Honourable Quarrels*, London, printed by John Wolfe, 1595.

Scott, M. A., *Elizabethan Translations from the Italian*, Boston & New York, Houghton Mifflin, 1916.

Shelley, H. C., *Inns and Taverns of Old London*; http://www.buildinghistory.org/primary/inns/inns.shtml (accessed August 2013).

Silver, G., *Brief Instructions upon my Paradoxes of Defence*, in Matthey, C. G. R. (ed.), *The Works of George Silver: Comprising 'Paradoxes of Defence' and 'Bref Instructions upon my Paradoxes of Defence'*, London: George Bell, 1898.

Silver, G., *Paradoxes of Defence*, London, Edward Blount, 1599.

Smith, I., *Shakespeare's Blackfriars Playhouse*, New York, New York University Press, 1964.

Stephen, Sir L. and Lee, Sir S., *Dictionary of National Biography*, Vol. 17, London, Oxford University Press, 1967–8.

Stone, G. C., *A Glossary of the Construction, Decoration and Use of Arms and Armor: In All Countries and in All Times*, New York, Jack Brussell, 1961.

Stubbes, P. and Furnivall, F. J., *Phillip Stubbes's Anatomy of Abuses in England in Shakspere's Youth, A.D. 1583: Part II: The Display of Corruptions Requiring Reformation*, London, Trübner, 1882.

Thibault, G., *Academie de l'Espée*, Leyden, Elzeviers, 1628.

Wheatley, H. B., *London Past and Present: Its Histories, Associations, and Traditions, Based upon the Handbook of London by the late Peter Cunningham*, London, Murray, 1891.

Williams, R. (trans.), *The Nicomachean Ethics of Aristotle*, London, Longmans, Green, 1869.